IN THE AUTUMN OF LIFE

Luis Alonso Schökel

In the Autumn of Life

Biblical meditations
on Hope for the elderly

SP St Paul Publications

Original title: *Esperanza. Meditaciones Bíblicas para la tercera edad*
Copyright © 1991 Luis Alonso Schökel

Translated by Dinah Livingstone

Cover photograph by Edmund Nägele FRPS

St Paul Publications
Middlegreen, Slough SL3 6BT, United Kingdom

English translation copyright © St Paul Publications, UK 1991

ISBN 085439 375 7

Printed by The Guernsey Press Co. Ltd, Guernsey, C.I.

St Paul Publications is an activity of the priests and brothers
of the Society of St Paul who proclaim the Gospel through the
media of social communication

Contents

Introduction   7

PART I : Meditations on the psalms   9

Psalm 1 : Jesus Way and Life   11
Psalm 4 : Freedom of Spirit   14
Psalm 5 : Waiting for God   16
Psalm 6 : Be gentle with me, Lord   18
Psalm 8 : What is a human being?   19
Psalm 12 : The Lord is my shield   22
Psalm 13 : Longing for God   26
Psalm 16 : Union with God   28
Psalm 17 : Seeing God's face   31
Psalm 19 : Freedom and innocence   33
Psalm 23 : The Lord is my shepherd   35
Psalm 25 : God forgives and forgets   38
Psalm 27 : Put your hope in the Lord   41
Psalm 30 : The pendulum of life   45
Psalm 31 : The Lord is my refuge   48
Psalm 32 : The joy of being forgiven   51
Psalm 33 : Sing a new song   53
Psalm 34 : See how good the Lord is   57
Psalm 36 : God's unfailing love   59
Psalm 37 : Working and praying for justice   62
Psalm 38 : The trials of Job   65

Psalm 41 : Helping the helpless   69
Psalms 42-3: The pain of God's absence   72
Psalm 44 : The suffering Church   77
Psalm 45 : Let's go to a wedding   81
Psalm 47 : Drawing nearer to God   85
Psalm 49 : Freedom from mortality   89
Psalm 55 : A prayer for peace   95
Psalm 57 : A new dawn   98
Psalm 62 : Trust in God   101
Psalm 63 : God in all things   105
Psalm 65 : God's presence in the world   109
Psalm 67 : The power to bless   113
Psalm 71 : The gift of old age   114

PART II : Biblical portraits of old people   121

Simeon : Hope was his daily bread   123
Abraham : The first patriarch   132
Isaac : Father of two nations   137
Jacob : Mediator of divine blessings   141
Moses : Man with a mission   148
Barzillai : Sensible to the end   154
Ecclesiastes : The lightness of being   156
Hezekiah : God knows best   163
Groups of leaders : Praising God   170
Paul : Be acceptable to God at all times   182
Nicodemus : A new and everlasting life   186

Introduction

On one occasion God tells the prophet Jeremiah: Let them turn to you, do not you turn to them. And a bit later on he adds: If you get rid of the dross from the precious metal you will be my true mouthpiece.

As I do not have a prophetic vocation I have meditated on these words and I shall apply the first text to people of my own age, pilgrims who have travelled a long way along the road of life. I shall address them so that they address themselves to the word of God in the Bible. But if the Bible is precious metal, I hope my words will not be the dross; otherwise I would have to be silent and let the words of the Bible speak for themselves. But the Church's tradition assures me that it is legitimate and convenient to explain the biblical text in such a way that the Christian can come into personal contact with it. Knowing that if I just give references the reader will not look them up in the Bible, I have preferred to quote the relevant texts or summarise their context.

Although the book can be read straight through, I wrote it for meditation and contemplation. I prefer suggesting to spelling everything out, I am not afraid to repeat if the biblical text repeats, I prefer to write in short sentences even though the resulting style may sometimes sound a bit clipped. I give aphorisms which can be underlined and assimilated without haste. Those meditating can re-read the book or certain meditations they like best or find most appropriate. But what is important is that they should turn directly to the biblical texts.

My preference for the Old Testament is explained by

+ maxim or general principle expressed in a few words.

the fact that it is my special field; but I always allow it to lead to the New Testament. If any theme dominates these pages it is hope, one of the theological virtues. And if I need a motto, I take it from the liturgy:

We announce your death, we proclaim your resurrection, come Lord Jesus.

Luis Alonso Schökel
San Francisco, California
Feast of St Ignatius, 31 July 1990

Part I

Meditations on the psalms

Preliminary remarks

When we are about to recite or meditate on the psalms it is a good idea to remind ourselves of two things, the technical names of which are *prosopology* and *appropriation*.

Prosopon is a Greek word meaning person. A psalm may be recited by one or more persons, who are not usually the author. We must distinguish between the authorial 'I' and the 'I' in the poem. Although they sometimes coincide, for example in lyrical confessions, the author often puts words into someone else's mouth. It is highly probable that the author of Psalm 88 enjoyed good health, but the words of the psalm are uttered by a dying man. Some psalms put words into the mouth of David, a king, a sick person, a teacher, an innocent person unjustly persecuted. Defining the person or character speaking in a psalm is the object of prosopology. Prosopon is a term taken from the theatre: in a psalm someone addresses someone else, speaks about a third person, engages in dialogue...

The moment comes when I am the one to recite the psalm. So I need to appropriate its words and feelings. If I am a Christian, my act of appropriation is via that of Jesus when he prayed the psalms. A new person, Jesus, appropriated the psalms to himself in a suitable manner and henceforth the psalms were marked in a definite way. When he prays the psalms Jesus begins a new chapter of prosopology and appropriation. The ancient commentators make the distinctions by asking: In whose name is he speaking? In his own name? In the name of the Church, the suffering, those asking forgiveness?

In appropriating the psalm, I join in the game of prosopology. In a sense I become a character, even though not a fictitious one, and I bring my personality into it. I cannot get away from it and I do not want to. I can pray in my own name, in the name of the Church, in the name of a persecuted or suffering brother or sister. I always make the psalm my own and I am bound to give it my tone of voice, my feeling. Suppose that now I am praying the psalm as an old person within the Church. Well, some psalms are explicitly or implicitly spoken by old people. Others sound this way when we say them. We are not continually thinking about old age. We calmly live the age we are without having to be conscious of it all the time. A good commentary on the psalms will be useful to anyone who studies it and uses it. But in these pages I want to offer something specific to the elderly and that is why I am spelling it out. We can say simply: here I am before God; it is not necessary to say specifically each time: here is an old person before God.

Psalm 1
Jesus Way and Life

The first psalm is the entry gate to the psalter. This psalm has a meditative character (some say a wisdom character). It is formulated like a beatitude: 'Blessed is the one who...' It is about life's journey and final destination, in the form of general utterances. It sets out two opposite roads and destinations, the good and the evil with nothing in between. And it uses two simple plant images. It is not difficult for this psalm to be appropriated by an old person, who has already come a long way and feels near the final destination. Let us concentrate briefly on three elements.

It is traditional in our culture to consider life and behaviour as a *road*: straight or crooked, flat or steep, up or down. From youth onwards we know the general direction but we cannot foresee the whole journey. Perhaps we have found it hard to allow ourselves to be led by God. Nevertheless, at the end of so many days' journey we can define the road according to where it has led us: God has brought us here. Straightening the crooked, flattening the steep (Is 40). Although we sometimes strayed or got stuck, on the whole our direction has been forwards and upwards. But there is still an uphill stretch in front.

The road leads to a *destination*, which will be shared with many others. Because 'the LORD watches over the way of the righteous' to lead them to this destination, which is himself. But 'the way of the wicked is doomed.'

The book of Proverbs develops this theme, linking road with light:

> [4:18]The course of the righteous is like morning light,
> growing ever brighter until it is broad day.
> [19]The way of the wicked is like deep darkness,
> and they do not know what has been their downfall.

Although our destination is near there is still a last lap. There, says Proverbs:

> [4:25]Let your eyes look straight before you,
> fix your gaze on what lies ahead.

The third theme is the image of the *tree*, signifying the natural vitality of the just, nourished by the stream of the Law. Of course the tree's vigour is more like the vigour of youth. But Psalm 92 speaks of a vigour which belies age:

> [12]The righteous shall flourish like a palm tree,
> they grow tall as a cedar on Lebanon;
> [13]planted in the house of the LORD,
> and flourishing in the courts of our God,
> [14]they still bear fruit in old age;
> they are luxuriant, wide-spreading trees.

The palm tree and the cedar are two equally beautiful but very different trees. The palm tree is like a graceful fountain gushing out into a green circle; the cedar a mass of needles forming an irregular shape which achieves its own majestic harmony. Cedar and palm tree, mountain and plain. The important thing is that these trees are planted in the temple court and watered by its sacred fountain.

The Christian meditating on this psalm recalls that Jesus is the way and the life. Way between his first and his final coming for us to tread step by step. Life by meditation and the practice of his law, which is the law of love and the Spirit. Christian love is a source of vitality. We have known people devoted to works of charity who renewed their strength in spite of their years. In doing good to their neighbour they did not feel old. Christ, who is our way, is also our destiny. We must be transplanted into the house of the Lord.

Psalm 4
Freedom of Spirit

This psalm is usually recited in the office of Compline that follows Vespers, a prayer for going to bed. For the moment let us consider the two symbols of space and sleep. Sleep is presented as a real occurrence in the psalm, but a symbolic meaning is also suggested, which we prefer here.

> [2]When I was hard pressed you set me free...

> [8]Now in peace I shall lie down and sleep;
> for it is you alone, LORD, who let me live in safety.

The first verse refers symbolically to all tight spots, pressing difficulties, narrow escapes, close shaves etc. we have been in (plenty of metaphors to choose from here). The Lord has given us ease, room, space, especially in spiritual matters. Perhaps with the years the Lord has given us freedom to open up to the breadth of the Spirit so that we can move freely. Because prohibitions restrict, laws constrict (from the Latin *stringere,* to squeeze), there are strict superiors. We need room for sorting ourselves out, we need to cultivate a broad gaze and open ourselves to a wide mental horizon. When we are old we are threatened by many things. There are old people who seem to shrivel like currants, others seem to be operating at last in four-dimensional space. The worm wriggling in the two dimensions of breadth and length inhabits a flattened universe. The bird flies in three

14

dimensions. The spirit seeks the fourth dimension. But don't we ourselves restrict and squeeze out the Spirit? Let us be as elastic as a balloon: allow the Spirit to fill us and swell our capacity from within.

When I was hard pressed you set me free. Do not let me submit to pressure again. Give me your ease and your ever-expanding space. Let my dimensions be *'the breadth and length and height and depth'* of Jesus Christ (Eph 3:18). Length we shall never come to the end of, breadth we shall never encompass, depth of mystery, height of destiny. Be my space in which 'I live and move and have my being' (Paul on the Areopagus, Acts 7:27).

The second symbol is that of sleep. Sleep is curiously ✳ ambivalent. It is rest but it makes us inactive; it closes our eyes and opens our imagination. It is present relief but an image and premonition of death. It is dreaming but that can become a nightmare. You, Lord, make me live in safety. You give me peace which enables me to fall asleep at once, without any worries, you free my sleep from nightmares.

And where does that leave the image of death? Jeremiah threatens in 51:57: *'they will sink into an unending sleep, never to wake again.'* I trust it will not be like this. When I fall into my last sleep you will come and wash over me until I wake to the endless morning, the reality which will be beyond all my dreams.

✳ co existence of 2 opposite emotions esp. love & hate. Towards the same object.

15

Psalm 5
Waiting for God

I am going to link a verse of this psalm with the previous meditation:

> [3]When I pray to you, LORD,
> in the morning you will hear me.
> I shall present my cause
> and keep watch.

Every morning that I wake I receive a gift of light and life. The sun has come punctually *'out of his chamber'*, ready to *'run his course'* (Ps 19), the earth has turned with precision, dawn has brought back shapes and colours to the world (Job 38;14). And here am I, Lord. The first thing I do this morning is tell you about my personal affairs and those of others I have made my own. *And I keep watch...* for you. I can do less and less but keeping watch is not a little thing. If I did not expect you to intervene — for now it is up to you — I should not keep watch. My life has become telling and keeping watch. I keep watch for your intervention in my affairs, but above all I keep watch for you: when will you come?

> [7]Through your great love I may come into your
> house.

I am keeping watch in the courtyard, in the porch, at the door. When will you open it for me? Not through my merits, Lord, but your great mercy. You are the master and have the key; *'evil can be no guest of yours'*, but your mercy will make me good and allow me to come in. Meanwhile I keep watch. Like the *girls who took their lamps and went out to meet the bridegroom:* even though the bridegroom delays, I shall be on the watch (Mt 25:1-13).

Psalm 6
Be gentle with me, Lord

Just one point for this psalm:

[7]Grief dims my eyes;
they are worn out because of all my adversaries.

Have you known people who have gone grey over-night, have grown years older in a few days? Sorrow makes them age in body and soul, and their eyes show it because they have been crying so much. Whether the fault is their own or someone else's, the effect is the same. Sorrow can be more bitter when we feel ourselves to blame and do not have the consolation of being innocent victims. But if I am guilty:

[2]LORD, do not rebuke me in your anger,
do not punish me in your wrath.

A child is told off with kindness and understanding so that he can accept being corrected. But I, LORD, am like a child again. I do not ask you not to tell me off or correct me. I only ask that you do so kindly, without anger. If I am so little I do not deserve God's anger. If I am weak I cannot bear it:

I said, 'LORD God, forgive, I pray you. How can Jacob survive? He is so small.' The LORD relented. 'This will not happen,' he said (Amos 7:2-3).

Let God turn to kindness:

Return, LORD, deliver me.

Psalm 8
What is a human being?

Verse 2 says in a probable translation (the Hebrew text is doubtful and disputed):

I shall praise Your Majesty above the heavens
with the mouth of a baby at the breast.

Well then? Must I miss out this beautiful psalm? Even though I have a few teeth missing (perhaps I have false ones), my mouth does not babble like a baby.

Must I think that Jesus did not recite this psalm? On the contrary, no one recited it better than he did. It is the easiest thing in the world to stammer. When we speak about God we humans only succeed in stammering. Moses protested: *'I have never been a man of ready speech... I am slow and hesitant.'* Jeremiah objects: *'Ah! Lord, I am not skilled in speaking; I am too young'* (1:6). If Jesus spoke intimately with his Father, this would not have been in purely human language.

Let us consider a more important aspect of the child: its capacity for wonder and amazement. The author of this psalm has contemplated the wonder of the starry sky, 'the work of God's fingers.' This childlike wonder is shared by many without any particular education. However little they know or reflect, they find the starry heavens wonderful and inexplicable. If they are believers they praise God for it. But we are adults. We have studied basic astronomy and later we read books or articles about discoveries and theories of astrophysics:

dwarf stars, doubles, reds, novas and supernovas, galaxies, pulsars... Can we marvel like children? Proportionally we have much more to admire. That the supernova now apparent in a known and described zone of the sky exploded seventy thousand years ago? Doesn't the distance make us giddy? The starry universe we know is much more wonderful than that observed by the ignorant child or the ancient author of Psalm 8. If I can contemplate the sky in ecstasy and wonder, I can praise God with a child's mouth. And I can ask with more clarity and gratitude:

> [4]What is a frail mortal, that you should be mindful
>   of him,
> a human being, that you should take notice of him?

Have I seriously considered what a human being is? I have studied anthropology. Perhaps I have divided it into anatomy, physiology and psychology. Perhaps I added history and sociology. But have I seriously considered what a human being is? A human being is asking what a human being is. Anyone who does not ask is not a real human being. So is the child, that great asker of questions a real human being? Let us say that he is on the way to becoming one if he is learning to question himself, or rather to look inwards and ask who he is. And I think an old person has many questions to ask, because some supposed certainties have been upset and questions have re-emerged. Among all the questions perhaps this is the main one: What is a human being? Particularly because God comes into the question *'that you should be mindful of him... that you should take notice of him?* Who has taken notice of me in every one of my million heartbeats? God. What *is a human being, that you should take notice of him?*

If I do not find an answer to my question, I turn to an image of the child Jesus in Mary's arms. Perhaps he can tell me what a human being is: discovering, as in a new Genesis, that the world is good, trying out human words in his mouth. We ask about human beings in order to know Jesus and ask about Jesus in order to know what a human being is. Thus each answer gives rise to another question. *'Your eyes do not grow tired of seeing or your ears of hearing'*, says Ecclesiastes. Will the mind grow tired of asking what a human being is?

Psalm 12
The Lord is my shield

Are we tired of words, fed up with them? It is not surprising. We are sick of grand words, because we have already assimilated so many, and we are tired of having to learn new words. We are fed up with empty or useless words because they befog us and deafen us. We are also increasingly besieged by images, through television and illustrated papers and books, but words still overwhelm us. The politician takes care of his image — but this image is largely made up of words. If advertising continues to lie, at least by exaggerating, it is because people believe it. If politicians go on lying in their promises, it is because people want to believe. At our age many have given up or become sceptical: it is not unreasonable to mistrust so many words.

Psalm 12 mentions one type of lie: duplicity of heart, which means lying on purpose, using deception as an offensive weapon. Adulation or flattery to curry favour or to damage someone else. Vain or arrogant proclamation of our own merits, boasting. And above all, language as the supreme instrument of power. This is how the list reads in the psalm text:

²One lies to another:
both talk with smooth words, but with duplicity in
   their hearts.
³May the LORD make an end of such smooth words,
and the tongue that talks so boastfully!
⁴They say, 'By our tongues we shall prevail.
With words as our ally, who can master us?'

It is not difficult to find modern examples. The politician promises what he cannot and does not intend to fulfil. Advertising appeals to all the senses, heightened by imagination, to persuade people to buy the product. Sometimes the assault is subliminal and difficult to guard against. Artists and sportsmen glory in being top and claim real or imaginary merits. And above all the media are an instrument of power. Anyone who controls the media controls the market and public opinion: *By our tongues we shall prevail*. It is extremely difficult to defend ourselves. We are citizens besieged in societies calling themselves free. The reason it is so difficult to defend ourselves from external power is that we are the enemy's accomplices. The besiegers can count on a fifth column. Why does deception recur so constantly? Because we want to be deceived. Why is the hidden lie so effective? Because people believe it. When they have been deceived again and again, why do they not finally learn? Because they want and need to believe it. Of course it is not always this way: there are honest and critical informers. Their help is precious for those who wish to receive it. But it is not always easily recognised.

In the Old Testament, in the wake of genuine prophets there arise false prophets, the bane of prophets like Micah, Jeremiah or Ezekiel. Jeremiah denounces them in his invective in chapter 23:

[14]Adulterers and hypocrites. They encourage
   evildoers
so that no one turns back from sin.
[21]I did not send these prophets, yet they went in
   haste;
I did not speak to them, yet they prophesied.
[22]But if they had stood in my council
they would have proclaimed my words to my
   people

and turned them from their evil ways and their evil
doings.
¹⁶Do not listen to what is prophesied to you by the
prophets who buoy you up with false hopes;
they give voice to their own fancies; it is not the
LORD's words they speak.

Ezekiel analyses the phenomenon and finds cases in
which the false prophet actually believes in the product
of his fantasy and hopes it will be fulfilled.

The vision is false, the divination a lie! They claim, 'It
is the word of the LORD,' when it is not the LORD who has
sent them, yet they expect him to confirm their prophe-
cies! (13:6)

Let us return to Psalm 12, which is thoroughly topical
in its general denunciations. How can there be a change?
Simple:

⁷The words of the LORD are unalloyed;
silver refined in a crucible, gold purified seven
times over.

God's word is given to us in scripture, the Old and
New Testament and the word of the Spirit speaking
within us.

So why do I spin out my words instead of just letting
the Bible speak directly? Wouldn't it be better to keep
quiet and just hand over the book of psalms for prayer
and meditation? Perhaps our words may serve to lead the
reader by the hand to the sanctuary of the Word. If this is
so, our words will fulfil their purpose when they cease,
when the moment of truth comes, that is, when the reader
or meditator remains alone and in silence with God's
word. The reader should carry on until you feel for
yourself that *'the words of the LORD are true words.'*
Jeremiah confesses (15:16):

When I received your words I devoured them;
your word was my joy and my delight.

God orders Ezekiel to eat the scroll which has on it
the message he is to proclaim (3:3): 'I ate it and it tasted
as sweet as *honey to me.*' So let the reader not just go on
listening to me talking but eat and savour the word of
God. Not forgetting this twelfth psalm's energetic
ending:

⁷LORD, you are our protector,
and will for ever guard us from such people.
⁸The wicked parade about,
and what is of little worth wins general esteem.

Psalm 13
Longing for God

About this psalm we must speak little and quickly, because it is a prayer of impatience. Children and old people are impatient, each in their own way. The child wants to hurry his life along: everything must be now at once. Old people mind any interruption of their routine, because they are losing their capacity to react and adapt. So what is the impatience this psalm is talking about? Let us read it:

> [1]How long, LORD, will you leave me forgotten,
> how long hide your face from me?
> [2]How long must I suffer anguish in my soul,
> grief in my heart day after day?
> How long will my enemy lord it over me?

So what impatience do we feel when we make this psalm our own? Paul said, *'My own desire is to depart and be with Christ,'* but he added, *'but for your sake the greater need is for me to remain in the body'* (Phil 1:23; see the sketch on Paul below). We hear that people who have undergone a near-death experience do not want to return. They want to stop themselves being brought back to life and if they do return it is with a serene longing for the other life. The saints give us another version: 'I live without living in myself and I expect so high a life that I die because I do not die.'

This leaves us with another important verse of the psalm:

[3]Look now, Lord my God, and answer me.
Give light to my eyes lest I sleep the sleep of death.

Do not deliver me Lord from sleep, do not deliver me
from death. Deliver me from a mortal sleep, from death
that dissolves me. Do not deliver me from dreaming of
you or from a death which is a tunnel or bridge to your
kingdom. Deliver me by your sleep from my delusions,
deliver me by death from my mortality:

[5]As for me, I trust in your unfailing love;
my heart will rejoice when I am brought to safety.
[6]I shall sing to the Lord
for he has granted all my desire.

Psalm 16
Union with God

If Psalm 13 is a prayer of impatience, Psalm 16 is a prayer of intimacy with God. The beginning of the text is very difficult. We can imagine it to be a profession of loyalty by a Levite on the day of his dedication or a priest on the day of his ordination. He professes loyalty to the Lord his God. He renounces all other gods and officially places himself under God's wing. Priests and Levites do not have a family landholding to live off. They are like guests or tenants of the temple where the Lord provides them with board and lodging. These everyday goods are a symbol and pledge of the higher good, which is daily being with God. Job recalled nostalgically *the days of my autumn when God was intimate in my tent*' (Job 29:4). The priest is an intimate in God's tent. Where are we? For a Christian intimacy with God is not a matter of space or place or time. Whether or not we are priests, we are in the autumn or winter of life and can aspire to intimacy with God. Although it is difficult to describe what this means the psalmist ventures to suggest certain aspects:

> [7]I shall bless the LORD who has given me counsel:
> in the night he imparts wisdom to my inmost being.
> [8]I have set the LORD before me at all times:
> with him at my right hand I cannot be shaken.

Let others learn from books or teachers, I have the Lord as my teacher and personal counsellor. In the silence of the night and when sleep comes the Lord instructs me. When my subconscious opens its doors, it can let in the Lord's suggestions. When consciousness is awake by day, I place the LORD before me. He is my wisdom and stability.

And what will become of the future? The psalmist makes a prodigious leap, which appears to take him into the New Testament. Or else he utters words which say more than he knows. Words which we can utter in full knowledge of their meaning. One who has lived intimately with God cannot perpetually be a citizen of the kingdom of death:

9Therefore my heart is glad
and my spirit rejoices,
my body too rests unafraid;
10for you will not abandon me to Sheol
or suffer your faithful servant to see the pit.
11You will show me the path of life;
in your presence is the fullness of joy,
at your right hand are pleasures for evermore.

These words gain new scope when they are uttered by Christ and then by the Christian in union with him. Christ passed through death but he did not fall under its dominion. He entered the sepulchre as a passing guest, for two nights, *like a traveller breaking his journey to find a night's lodging'*, as Jeremiah puts it (14:8). Through the tunnel of death he passes to the path of life. Now Jesus Christ is seated at the Father's right hand, enjoying his perpetual blessing. This fact has changed life's meaning: now its meaning is not a descent but an ascent. Jesus Christ wishes to share his life and joy with us. We read in John 16:

²⁰Though you will be plunged in grief, your grief will be turned to joy...

²²For the moment you are sad, but I shall see you again and then you will be joyful and no one shall rob you of your joy.

A Hebrew proverb says: *'Even amid laughter the heart weeps and joy ends in affliction.'* The words of Christ, God's Wisdom, turn this proverb upside down, so that it could say: 'Even amid weeping the heart laughs and sorrow ends in joy.' Perpetual joy in your presence, Lord, is still in the future for me. But this is anticipated now by a hope that pours into my heart and fills it, overflows and floods through my body. Because *you will fill me* Lord, and I know it, you are already filling me. When I come to the end of the *path of life*, you will have to broaden my capacity a great deal so that I can share the *joy at your right hand.*

Psalm 17
Seeing God's face

This psalm is the prayer of an innocent person who is unjustly accused and who appeals to God's judgment and proclaims his innocence. This is the meaning of *'my plea is just'* in the last verse. This is not boasting about personal merits. A guilty person could not stand before God, because *no godless person may appear before him* (Job 13:16). And if he were guilty, his declaration of innocence would make the crime worse. It is not so and God knows the depths of the heart:

> [3]You have tested my heart
> and watched me all night long;
> you have assayed me and found no malice in me.

Therefore the psalmist can say in the last verse and we can appropriate this for ourselves:

> [15]My plea is just: may I see your face
> and be blest with a vision of you when I awake.

So what is he saying? When Moses asked, *'Show me your glory'*, God answered: *'My face you cannot see, for no mortal may see me and live'* (Ex 33:20). It is true, we could not bear the vision of God in this life, we have to pass over to the other side to *'gaze our fill upon him'* . Ecclesiastes said: *our eyes have had enough of seeing'* (1:8), but he was thinking about the things in this world. There we shall gaze our fill without ever having enough.

We will never be sated. 'Whoever feeds on me will hunger for more; whoever drinks from me will thirst for more' (Ecclus 24:21).

'When I awake', says the psalm. Paul advises us:

It is high time for you to wake out of sleep, for deliverance is nearer to us now than it was when first we believed. It is far on in the night; day is near. Let us therefore throw off the deeds of darkness and put on the armour of light. (Rom 13:11)

The Letter to the Ephesians expresses it thus:

Awake, sleeper,
rise from the dead,
and Christ will shine upon you (5:14).

We may also recall the Lord's magnificent dialogue with Jerusalem in Isaiah 51-52:

She: Awake, awake! Arm of the LORD, put on your strength; awake as you did in days of old, in ages long past! (51:9).

He: Arouse yourself; rise up, Jerusalem! (51:17).
Awake, awake, Zion, put on your strength; Jerusalem, Holy City, put on your splendid garments! (52:1).

Finally, speaking of the face, we feel we must mention St John of the Cross:

Oh silver fountain,
that you would in your surfaces of crystal
form me the reflection
of the face for which I long,
which I carry printed on my soul!

Psalm 19
Freedom and innocence

The final part of the above psalm shows that we do not claim total innocence before God but that we are referring to a particular accusation. In Psalm 19 the psalmist sings the qualities of the law and the LORD's commandments *more to be desired than gold, pure gold in plenty, sweeter than honey dripping from the comb.* Then he looks within himself and realises that his behaviour does not correspond to the enthusiasm he has expressed. Examining his conduct in the light of these precepts he discovers three sins, two present ones and a possible one in the future. They are not different in kind or in their object, but are distinguished by attitude and awareness.

> [11]It is through them that your servant is warned;
> in obeying them is great reward.
> [12]Who is aware of his unwitting sins?
> Cleanse me of any secret faults.
> [13]Hold back your servant also from wilful sins,
> lest they get the better of me.
> [14]Then I shall be blameless,
> innocent of grave offence.

First there are *unwitting* sins, or acts of which we are not fully aware or responsible for. Nevertheless we accept limited responsibility, in order to educate our awareness. We do not let up on our vigilance as if all the danger had passed, we do not cultivate permanent distraction claiming we are tired. We recognise this smudged margin to our conscience, this reek of our sinful condition.

Secondly, *hidden faults:* hidden from me but nothing can be hidden from God. Sometimes they are not hidden through weakness but because it suits us. Evil is the damp basement we do not want to go down into or put a light in so that we can see there. Our conscious mind keeps watch at the door so that our ghosts do not get out and come up to visit us. We are afraid to see and confess what lies below our consciousness. And if anything surprises us, we know the mechanism to neutralise it: rationalisation, seeking reasons to justify and excuse it; by sublimating it, disguising it as noble and altruistic. A proverb says: 'The LORD shines into a person's soul, searching out his inmost being' (Prov 20:27). Let us recognise, at least in general, *what is hidden from us —* that is not hidden from God — and let us pray: 'Cleanse me of any secret fault.'

Thirdly comes sin committed on purpose, *assuming* the right to decide against God's authority. We assume an authority that does not belong to us: authority against God. Thus we claim to be masters but make ourselves slaves. Because sin is a power that wants to dominate us (Gen 4:7). And John says: *'Everyone who commits sin is a slave'* (Jn 8:34). At the end of John's first letter we read:

'If anyone sees a fellow-Christian committing a sin which is not a deadly sin, he should intercede for him, and God will grant him life — that is, to those who are not guilty of deadly sin. There is such a thing as deadly sin, and I do not suggest that he should pray about that. Although all wrongdoing is sin, not all sin is deadly sin' (5:16,17).

Lord, I am not and cannot be innocent. Absolve me from my secret faults, guard me from arrogance and then I shall be free and innocent.

Psalm 23
The Lord is my shepherd

This psalm is a favourite of all ages and in all sorts of cultures. We have prayed this psalm countless times for many years and we can go on doing so without thinking about our age. Let us have another look at it. The poem consists of two complementary images. In the first God is the shepherd, in the second he is a host. The first image generates a number of symbols: resting on green grass, water restoring strength, a guide along the way. The second offers complementary symbols: safe hospitality, food and drink, anointing oil, an escort for the journey. Let us look at two moments on the road. In verse 4 it is dark night and the road runs through a valley. Although they do not know the way, the sheep do not get frightened or lost. They hear the rhythmic tapping of the shepherd's crook on the stones, perhaps they feel the touch of his staff guiding them. At this dark moment the psalm, which up till now has spoken of God in the third person, addresses him directly:

> 4Even were I to walk through of valley of deepest darkness
> I should fear no harm, for you are with me;
> your shepherd's staff and crook comfort me.

Now turn to verse 6 at the end of the psalm. After having enjoyed a moment of hospitality, I set out on the journey escorted by two of the Lord's servants, Goodness and Mercy: *Goodness and mercy will follow me all the days of my life.* So we come to the journey's end, a perpetual home: *And I shall dwell in the house of the* LORD *always*.

Journey, hospitality, journey, home. It is easy to say these verses at any moment in our lives for we are always on a journey. Brief stops to eat and drink, like Elijah, to rest and refresh ourselves with ointment. We cannot drag ourselves along the road when we are exhausted; we cannot make these stopping places our final home. Although the Lord is our host, who restores us at his table with his food and drink, although he offers his protection *against enemies*, we are not yet finally *in the house of the Lord*.

There is still some way to go. Maybe there is still another whole new stage of the journey. That may depend on us. Suppose our situation has changed at work, at home. We have more time, fewer responsibilities. What do we do with our time and talents? With the knowledge we have accumulated and skills acquired? This may be the moment to sit down and plan for the future. We may or may not need further education or re-training. Let us plan what we can do for ourselves and for others. For ourselves, so many things that we could not do for lack of time. For others too. In our present society, especially in cities, one of the things that is most precious, because of its scarcity, is time. What a lot of things we deny ourselves and others for lack of time. A lot of precious time is wasted in travelling and waiting. In the little free time we have we feel like relaxing and being entertained. Well, now a period is beginning in which we are going to have a wealth of time, more than other people. There is still a world for us to discover and conquer. Let us look at Elijah. Hounded to death by Jezebel, he flees to the south. He reaches the frontier of the city and the desert. He leaves his servant, goes on alone. He then prays God to die. He is worn out and sick of living:

'It is enough,' he said, 'now LORD, take away my life, for I am no better than my fathers before me' (1 Kings 19:4).

God sends him an angel with water and cake. The prophet eats and falls asleep. But the angel wakes him and orders him to go on, because he still has a long journey ahead of him. The best and most difficult part is still ahead: going up the mountain to meet God. As in Psalm 23 the halt has been temporary in order to regain strength and go on to the next important stage.

I am about to set out on a new stage, Lord. Let me feel your presence and the touch of your staff if the road is dark. Let your *goodness and mercy escort me all the days of my life*. Although I miss many things, I lack nothing because you go with me. Although my hair is grey and perhaps my life is grey, you lead me in green pastures. Although my feelings and imagination may dry up, you lead me by calm waters. If I am hungry, you sit me at your table. If I am thirsty, you pass me your cup. After visiting you I can begin a new stage — the last but one. Because the final one will be *dwelling in your house always*. See also Psalm 84.

Psalm 25
God forgives and forgets

'*Do not remember the sins and offences of my youth.*' They say that old people live on their memories. As if through memory one could relive what one is no longer able to do. In memory past events are transfigured or disfigured. Imagination recalls certain significant features of the old situation. Emotion wells up as if from a spring and waters the spirit. It is the past feeling or its equivalent, with added tenderness and nostalgia. It can be a delicious, slightly intoxicating brew. When two old friends from school or university meet after many years, they enjoy remembering the old days. It is odd how the old feel tenderly towards their grandchildren or children in general. It is as if they felt sympathy with the child they used to be themselves. That rather sad child who felt painfully misunderstood. Many years later they finally find someone who understands and sympathises — the old person that they will be, that they now are. A mysterious meeting with oneself. Youth also needs this understanding and sympathy. Meeting one's own youth is probably less tender, more severe. Do the old perhaps reproach their own youth with what they do not like in the young people they know now? Still, youth recalled can also make us nostalgic. Maturity rather less so.

In this exercise of memory which threatens to take up somewhat too much of our time do we leave any space for our sins? Machado said: 'Oh that I could dream the youth I did not live.' Let us say: 'Can anyone put right a youth that was misspent?' From time to time a general reminder of our sins, the single memory of some particular ones, can be an exercise in humility and gratitude. Because it is not so much a matter of feeling we are sinners than of feeling we are forgiven. This feeling also mingles sorrow with comfort.

The psalmist in Psalm 25 projects his human experience of remembering onto God and asks him not to remember the sins of his youth as if God was co-extensive with human time. If God is going to exercise memory, let its object be not human sins but the calls on his goodness.

> [6]Remember, LORD, your tender care
> and love unfailing,
> for they are from of old.
> [7]Do not remember the sins
> and offences of my youth,
> but remember me in your unfailing love,
> in accordance with your goodness, LORD.

When he mentions *sins and offences* he remembers them as a whole. When he prays God not to remember them he begs for forgiveness again. Un-remember is *a-mnistia* in Greek. And if the memory of a certain sin torments me, God's forgiveness and forgetting will comfort me:

> [16]Turn to me and show me your favour,
> for I am lonely and oppressed.
> [17]Relieve the troubles of my heart
> and lead me out of my distress.
> [18]Look on my affliction and misery
> and forgive me every sin.

If we know and feel we are forgiven we do not have to

keep remembering our sins. It is more important to go ahead along the right road, the road we have to travel:

4Make your paths known to me, LORD;
teach me your ways.
5Lead me by your faithfulness and teach me,
for you are God my saviour.
8The LORD is good and upright;
therefore he teaches sinners the way they should go.
9He guides the humble in right conduct,
and teaches them his way.

Psalm 27
Put your hope in the Lord

Sometimes we boast of our bravery not really to say how brave we are but how brave we should like to be. As if by dint of proclaiming our courage we manage to master our fears. Meanwhile our fears still lie in wait ready for next time. Fear is still there and we want to overcome it. We deny it in order to make it cease to be. But our words do not destroy our fears. We are not creators in reverse who can say: 'Let fear not exist', and fear ceases to exist. This is what seems to be happening to the psalmist in Psalm 27:

> [1]...whom should I fear... of whom then should I go
>   in dread?
> [3]Should an army encamp against me,
> my heart would have no fear;
> if armed men should fall upon me,
> even then I would be undismayed.

Of course this sketch is not complete because I have mentioned two factors and left out the third by putting dots. The third factor which enables us really to overcome fear is the Lord present to help us:

> [1]The LORD is my light and my salvation ;
> whom should I fear?
> The LORD is the stronghold of my life;
> of whom then should I go in dread?

This is how the psalm begins. Throughout the Old Testament when God presents himself to a human being, one of his most frequent greetings is: 'Do not be afraid.' Do not be afraid of me, who am God, or of human beings who are flesh, grass:

Why then fear man who must die,
who must perish like grass? (Is 51:12)

Fear belongs to human nature because it is linked to the instinct of self-preservation. But it is also human to overcome fear, by reason. In the book of Wisdom, chapter 17, the author tries to describe and analyse fear, the fear of the guilty:

'Thinking that their secret sins might escape detection beneath a dark pall of oblivion, they lay in disorder, dreadfully afraid, terrified by apparitions. Not even the dark corner that hid them offered refuge from fear, but loud unnerving noises resounded about them, and phantoms with faces firm and downcast passed before their eyes. No fire, however intense, was strong enough to give them light, nor were the brilliant flaming stars adequate to pierce that hideous darkness. There shone on them only a terrifying blaze of no human making, and in their panic they thought the real world even worse than the sight their imagination conjured up. The tricks of the sorcerer's art failed, and their boasted wisdom was exposed and put to shame; for those who professed to drive out fear and trouble from sick souls were themselves sick with dread that made them ridiculous. Even if there was nothing frightful to terrify them, yet having once been scared by the advance of the vermin and this hissing of the serpents, they collapsed in terror, even refusing to look upon the air from which there could be no escape. For wickedness proves a cowardly thing when condemned by an inner witness, and in the grip of conscience gives way to foreboding of disaster. Fear is nothing but an abandonment of the aid that reason affords; and hope, defeated by this inward weakness, capitulates in ignorance of the cause by which the torment comes' (Wis 17:3-13).

And the rest of the chapter continues in this vein.

Every age has its fears, because fear is our companion throughout life. Now we laugh at ourselves indulgently for our childhood fears. The adolescent and young person tries not to feel fear or at least not to show it: 'You're scared!' 'What, me? You'll see.' Perhaps when we are adults we achieve a certain balance in the mastery of our fears or at least learn to live with them. Old age also has to cope with its fears. It is as if they had been waiting for you at this late stage. 'At last you have arrived, we were waiting for you. Here we are to go with you, you can't get away from us.' How does an old person cope with fears?

When we examine our conscience we do not usually survey our fears. Why? We examine and confess our evil desires: greed, ambition, lust. Desires are for things that seem good to us, fears are of things that we think are bad. The Stoics drew a square for the passions: desire for a good we do not possess, fear of an evil that is threatening us, enjoyment of a good we possess, the pain of evil that we suffer. In our spiritual life we pay quite a lot of attention to desires: 'I have had evil desires.' We also note how we have not tolerated annoying things: 'I have been impatient.' Sometimes we give fleeting attention to things we have enjoyed: 'I was glad about someone else's suffering.' So what is left for fears? God tells Jeremiah: *'Brace yourself, Jeremiah... when you confront them do not let your spirit break, or I shall break you before their eyes'* (Jer 1:17). And we read in the gospel: 'Do not fear those who kill the body, but cannot kill the soul' (Mt 10:28). Once we have recognised and confessed our fears, we gather strength to overcome well-founded fears and reject those that are unfounded. I knew someone who was afraid of things that might happen. I argued that we should only fear what probably will happen, not just anything possible but the fairly probable. To overcome fear above all we have the resource of prayer. This is where Psalm 27 comes in. If his parents were still alive, the psalmist must have been young or at least not old. But the reference may simply be a manner of speaking:

> [10]Though my father and mother forsake me,
> the LORD will take me into his care.

We heard the psalmist say: 'Lord, I seek your face, do not hide your face from me.' Now let us hear what the Lord replies:

> [14]Wait for the LORD; be strong and brave,
> and put your hope in the LORD.

So against fear we have hope. And what better hope can there be than that in verse 4:

> One thing I ask of the LORD,
> it is the one thing I seek:
> that I may dwell in the house of the LORD
> all the days of my life.

Psalm 30
The pendulum of life

Human life is like a pendulum swinging. Ecclesiastes gives us a list of fourteen swings:

> 3:2 A time to be born and a time to die;
> a time to plant and a time to uproot;
> 4 time to weep and a time to laugh;
> a time for mourning and a time for dancing;
> 6 time to seek and a time to lose;
> a time to keep and a time to discard;
> 8 time to love and a time to hate;
> a time for war and a time for peace.

Psalm 30 puts it like this: anger and favour, afternoon and morning, crying and rejoicing, mourning and dancing, sackcloth and party. Of all the oppositions the most radical in the psalm is that between life and death; being born and dying; in Ecclesiastes: being born to live, living to die. There is no doubt about the direction of the movement in Ecclesiastes. But what about the psalm?

The psalmist has looked death in the face. He had one foot in the grave when he was pulled out alive. It was like being born again. He despaired and he was saved so now he enjoys life because he can contrast it. Now rejoicing, dancing and partying dominate his thoughts because just being alive is a party. He already knew this but he caught a glimpse of death and felt the silence of those who do not praise God or give thanks. He too was struck dumb but he has regained his speech. How wonderful to be able to speak and give thanks to God, to proclaim his faithfulness, *to sing with all his soul, for ever.*

Really? What does for ever mean? For the Old Testament psalmist it means throughout life. And how much longer will his life last? After crying comes rejoicing, after evening and night comes the dawn. But a night will fall for him which will have no dawn. *I felt secure and said: I can never be shaken.* A vain thought; because never means as long as I am alive, and living is going towards death. This is the direction in which the psalm moves for the Old Testament psalmist.

But when a Christian says this psalm the meaning is reversed. With Christ's death and resurrection there was a great revolution. After the nightfall of death comes the dawn of resurrection, a day which will not set.

> The sun will no longer be your light by day,
> nor the moon shine on you by night;
> the LORD will be your everlasting light,
> your God will be your splendour.
> Never again will your sun set
> nor your moon withdraw her light;
> but the LORD will be your everlasting light
> and your days of mourning will be ended.
>
> (Is 60:19-20)

We hear an echo of this proclamation in Revelation 21:23:

> The city did not need the sun or the moon to shine on it, for the glory of God gave it light, and its lamp was the Lamb.

How would Jesus speak verse 9?

What profit is there in my death,
in my going down to the pit?
Can the dust praise you?
Can it proclaim your truth?

It is true that dust cannot give thanks to God. But Jesus does not turn to dust. His death and his going down in to the grave are profit for God because they are of profit to us. What do you gain from my death? You gain a people for yourself, we gain liberation from corruption. Even though we turn to dust, we shall return and give thanks for ever. Strange profit that makes us celebrate a death.

Medicine, hygiene, modern surgery mean that the cure described in the psalm can happen without miracles: *LORD my God, I cried to you and you healed me.* Life's pendulum which was about to stop starts up again. Again it swings between crying and rejoicing, mourning and dancing. Perhaps now the rhythm is different. Once again I can praise God and I have a new reason for giving thanks. Lord, I have many more things to thank you for, I need a long time to give you thanks. I need all time or time without end because every song of mine in your honour is a new grace of yours. Lord, do not leave me in the dust. I need to give thanks to you for ever.

Psalm 31
The Lord is my refuge

This psalm is not talking about evils that may come which frighten us, or past evils overcome for which we rejoice, but present evils which are with us now. The psalm describes them thus:

> [9]Be gracious to me LORD, for I am in distress
> and my eyes are dimmed with grief.
> [10]My life is worn away with sorrow
> and my years with sighing;
> through misery my strength falters
> and my bones waste away.
> [11]I am scorned by all my enemies,
> my neighbours find me burdensome,
> my friends shudder at me,
> when they see me on the street they turn away
>   quickly.
> [12]Like the dead I have passed out of mind;
> I have become like some article thrown away.

Hostility is a way of taking our neighbour into account: 'If they think of me as a rival, this means I still count.' Being forgotten is painful, but it can lead to an inner refuge where you can live serenely. But do not old people exaggerate when they see nothing but neglect and hostility towards them? Perhaps these are imaginary, or perhaps the old people provoke them by their bad temper. It may also be that old rivalries now find an opportunity to strike. There is still another severe suffering: 'I am like something thrown away.' This is especially painful for anyone who has been a worker, creative artist, or an important person in a business or institution. It is painful if you are still doing your job because others who want your job do not recognize your ability. If you can no longer do it, it is painful because your rivals are right. Without a job you cannot help comparing what you are now to what you once were and it is painful to be useless now, a burden. Is there anything else? How does God treat me in this situation?

23In sudden alarm I said,
I am shut out from your sight.

If I am suffering in this way, it is because God is no longer concerned about me. Perhaps he is punishing me, or is reproaching me for my laziness in prayer. But it is not laziness, it is because I feel tired and weak. Am I becoming useless, an article thrown away, even in my dealings with God?

Nevertheless the psalmist produces a long psalm, repeating, stressing his point. He does not give any signs of tiredness. Let us consider first a great contrast. An old person feels worn out, decayed.

2Be to me a rock of refuge,
a stronghold to keep me safe.
3You are my rock and my stronghold...

The contrast does not depress, but is a comfort, shown by the possessive adjectives *my* rock and *my* stronghold. Hence the trust expressed in the admirable verse:

15My fortunes are in your hand.

We say in general terms, 'we are in God's hands.' I find the way the psalm puts it more expressive: *my fortunes* are in God's hands (in Hebrew *'ittotay* = my hours, my moments). We saw Ecclesiastes' list of fourteen opposite pairs for these moments or fortunes. Because *all my fortunes are in your hands, therefore*

[14]In you, LORD, I put my trust;
I say, you are my God.

One verse remains expressing a parallel thought to verse 15. It has special importance because Luke quotes it as Jesus' last words: '*Into your hands I commend my spirit*' (v 5). I commend or commit, I entrust my spirit, breath or life to you, leave it in your hands, your power, at your disposal. When Jesus gives up his life he deposits it in the Father's hands… and he loses, he dies. This is the paradox: the Father returns the deposit in the form of new life. In Jesus' mouth the psalmist's words change meaning, since the psalmist prayed, hoped he would not lose his life. You *deliver me LORD, you God of truth… you have cared for me in my distress… Save me in your unfailing love* (vv. 5,7,16). These phrases sound different when Jesus says them. And when the Christian prays this psalm he does so like Christ. Lord, while I live, *my fortunes are in your hands* and you deliver me from evils and dangers and give me space to move. When my last hour comes, Lord, I commit my life into your hands. Your faithfulness will be my joy, because I trust in you, Lord. From death's final power *save me in your unfailing love and let your face shine on your servant.*

Psalm 32
The joy of being forgiven

There is a blessing in not sinning and another in being forgiven. I am not thinking of the Pharisee who declares his exemplary blamelessness while the tax collector or publican proclaims himself a sinner. I am thinking of the blessing in Psalm 1, which consists in avoiding the wrong road and bad company. Let us compare these two blessings.

> 1:1Happy is the one who does not take the counsel of the wicked for a guide.

> 32:1Happy is he whose offence is forgiven.

Although we may not have made a habit of taking the wrong road, it is possible that we have taken a few wrong turnings, slipped up once or twice. Is it a calamity or a misfortune? A misfortune but not irremediable, because there is another blessing, as necessary in practice as the first:

> 1Happy is he whose offence is forgiven
> whose sin is blotted out!
> 2Happy is he to whom the LORD imputes no fault,
> in whose spirit there is no deceit.

We can remind ourselves briefly of sins in our lives, or glance at some of our darker moments. To the sadness of having committed these sins and being unable to undo them is added the joy of being forgiven. Forgiveness is not merited by our humble confession but a *gift* of God (for-give comes from give). Our humble confession is merely a condition for forgiveness:

> [5]I acknowledged my sin to you
> I no longer concealed my guilt,
> but said, I shall confess my offence to the LORD.

But do we need to tell God something he knows better and more thoroughly than we do ourselves? We need to confess *to clear our conscience*. We are not black holes from which nothing comes out. We must call to mind what God sees in us, and what we do not manage to see we should subject to *God's gaze*.

> You set our iniquities before you,
> our secret sins in the light of your presence
> > (Ps 90:8).

Feeling forgiven means recognising that we need forgiveness and therefore that we are sinners. The Christian must take up his cross every day and keep Christ's cross present. From this cross that presides over our life Jesus repeats every day: Forgive them! These words give us a share in a blessing.

Psalm 33
Sing a new song

This psalm invites us to *sing a new song*, as if the songs we sang before were used up or finished. Is it possible to sing a new song at this point? At this point in the psalter or this point in our lives?

There are people who like novelty, others prefer custom or routine. Jesus spoke of those who preferred the old wine, that is, what they have always been used to. Sometimes I wonder why we seek variety for our lunch whereas our breakfast is the same every day. In the morning we have a routine, at lunch time we seek novelty. Is it a question of age or temperament? Probably both, and perhaps our upbringing is a third factor. But we come across the paradox that some people are accustomed to seek novelty. Possibly old age inclines us more towards routine. But thinking of temperament Picasso said that someone who is young is young all their life. I would suggest to those of my age, 'the third age', that in ordinary and secondary things we rely on routine in order to free our strength and concentrate our attention on what is new every day.

In the order of praise, young and old are invited to sing a new song. To do this in a verse of a psalm seems like a contradiction or at least a fallacy. In fact if I spend years reciting this psalm it is not new for me. If I recite it again, I contradict its invitation. If I accept its invitation I have to seek or invent another song. Either the words or the music must change. That's it: if we alter our feeling, or understanding of the text and its symbols, we can sing a new song even with the same words and music:

> ¹Shout for joy in the Lord, you that are righteous,
> praise comes well from the upright.
> ²Give thanks to the LORD on the lyre;
> make music to him on the ten-stringed harp.
> ³Sing to him a new song;
> strike up with all your skill and shout in triumph.

Let us go on. What is the theme or reason for praise? One that suits a new song very well: *creation*. Nothing is so new as creation. It is an absolute beginning, the passing from not being to being.

> ⁶The word of the LORD created the heavens;
> all the host of heaven was formed at his command.
> ⁹For he spoke, and it was;
> he commanded, and there it stood.

But if creation is absolute newness, once it has happened it is no longer new. The people of Israel looked on the mountains as primordial and permanent. Now what exists is not new, it merely continues to be. The second time a song is sung it is not new.

This is not so for the Hebrews, or at least not for some of them. If the first chapter of Genesis gives the impression that by the sabbath the task of creation was finished and God's rest began, other texts speak of creation as something new in *history*, something that does not yet exist. A wonderful action can be called creation: the earth opening (Num 16:30), the final liberation of Israel (Ex 34:10); a new generation (Ps 102:19), life renewed on earth (Ps104:30). Second Isaiah, the prophet of the exile is a specialist on this theme, because he thinks of the coming repatriation and restoration of the Jews as a new creation. The Lord created the people. He affirms the new creation polemically:

> 48:7They were not created long ago, but in this very hour.
> Before today you had never heard of them.
> You cannot claim, I know them already.

At the end of the book of Isaiah God announces a completely new creation:

> 65:17See, I am creating new heavens and a new earth!

Although we have lived many years we have no right to become blasé: 'Seen everything, nothing new.' Isaiah forbids us. Those of us who lived during the Second Vatican Council and during the second half of 1989 in Europe cannot say that nothing new ever happens. And if we recognise God's hand in events, like a miracle or a new creation, we have material and reason for a new song. And there may be new events in our private lives too. A child born – a grandchild, a great nephew, a friend's child – is something new and wonderful. Forty years ago a science professor spoke to me of novas and supernovas as if they were new creative acts of God. I don't think that is the correct explanation today (or then). But it is true that it is not necessary to think of the act of creation as a single moment, the great initial explosion, big bang (which is being disputed again today). If God is outside time, his creative action can be contemporary with any moment and we can sing him a new song. And this goes for human history when human projects fail and God's plan is fulfilled:

[10]The LORD frustrates the purposes of nations;
he foils the plans of the peoples.
[11]But the LORD's own purpose stands for ever,
and the plans he has in mind endure for all
   generations.

Has the New Testament ceased to be new for us? Should we change the adjective? Anyone who meditates seriously on it will find it is always new. It too deserves a new song. Let us keep looking attentively to see what is new and keep our hearing tuned to sing the LORD a new song.

The seer in Revelation contemplating the final glory sings a new song:

I saw a new heaven and a new earth, for the first heaven and the first earth had vanished, and there was no longer any sea. I saw the Holy City, the new Jerusalem, coming down out of heaven from God, made ready like a bride adorned for her husband. I heard a loud voice proclaiming from the throne:

Now God has his dwelling with mankind!
He will dwell among them and they shall be his
   people,
and God himself will be with them.
He will wipe every tear from their eyes.
There shall be an end to death,
and to mourning and crying and pain,
for the old order has passed away.

The One who sat on the throne said, 'I am making all things new!'

For the past of creation and history, for the present in which we are living and the future we hope for, we sing the Lord a *new song*.

Psalm 34
See how good the Lord is

Is it true that as the years pass our senses fail or become dulled? Experience tells us so, but we usually apply this only to seeing and hearing. Speaking of Moses, Deuteronomy 34:7 tells us that at his death at the age of a hundred and twenty 'he had not lost his sight.' This is a legendary piece of information but it reveals a mentality shared by author and readers. And it is about Moses, an exceptional man. Speaking of a normal old person Ecclesiastes comments: 'What they look at through the window will become dim... The noise of the mill will cease': sight and hearing. Our other senses are also dulled (as Barzillai tells us): taste, smell, touch.

But there are inner senses of imagination and spirit, which do not grow dull with the years. Beethoven listened to his symphonies with his inner ear because his bodily ears were deaf. Spiritual masters refer to the inner senses in what they call the application of the senses. Psalm 34 speaks of them symbolically:

> [5]They who look to him are radiant with joy.
> [8]Taste and see that the LORD is good.

The first of these verses refers to sight and alludes to Moses' experience when he spoke with the Lord *face to face as a man speaks with his friend*. He came back *with his face radiant*. He had absorbed the light or glory of the Lord and it was reflected in his face. The psalm extends the privilege of Moses to all who go to the temple and want to repeat his experience.

The second of the above verses refers to the sense of taste. It does not invite us to savour the liturgical banquet — roast meat of sacrificed victims — but the Lord himself. As if letting him slowly penetrate us, we savour his exquisite taste. Eve ate the forbidden fruit and decided it tasted good. The book of Wisdom recalls the story of the manna:

16:20Your own people were given angels' food. You sent to them from heaven, without labour on their part, bread ready to eat, rich in every kind of delight and suited to every taste.

Ezekiel found God's word tasted sweet (Ezek 3:3) and Psalm 19 declares it is *sweeter than honey*. Psalm 34 offers much more: God himself as tasty spiritual manna. To taste him the spiritual senses do not grow dull in old age. The First Letter of Peter (2:3) quotes this verse of the psalm. The Letter to the Hebrews picks up the image:

For when people have once been enlightened, when they have tasted the heavenly gift and have shared in the Holy Spirit, when they have savoured the goodness of God's word...

In this way the world of our senses penetrates into the world of the Spirit. When he was dying John of the Cross heard a guitar playing and said: 'a better music sounded in my senses.' In his *Spiritual Canticle* he speaks of the 'inner cellar'. We sang the Lord a new song. Will he not now sing a new song to us?

Psalm 36
God's unfailing love

Before he approached the burning bush, Moses had to take off his shoes. No object made by human hands was to profane the holy place. Moses' bare skin touched the damp rough earth. Thus we too must rid ourselves of concepts and opinions in order to penetrate the world of symbols which Psalm 36 offers us.

6LORD, who saves man and beast,
7how precious is your unfailing love!

The first animals appeared on earth millions of years ago. You protected them, Lord! They grew and changed, enormous dinosaurs roamed the continents. You looked after them, Lord. Some species disappeared and others appeared, the dinosaurs were succeeded by mammals, you looked after them, Lord. Aquatic animals moved onto dry land, they grew feet, they grew wings, they flew. Whales which lived on dry land went into the sea. You, Lord, looked after every species. At the end of millions of years, human beings appeared and you, Lord, looked after them without ceasing to look after the animals. The human species also changed and diversified and spread over the earth. *And you Lord looked after humans and animals. How precious is your unfailing love, Oh God!* Unfailing love to all you have created but above all to humanity, your favourite, with whom you converse, the only one of your creatures to address you. For human beings you reserved special benefits.

This is God speaking to Job about the animals:

38:41who provides the raven with its quarry
when its fledglings cry aloud croaking for lack of
    food?
39:1Do you know when the mountain goats give
    birth?
Do you attend the wild doe when she is calving?
5Who has let the Syrian wild ass range at will
and given the Arabian wild ass its freedom?
6I have made its haunts in the wilderness
and its home in the saltings.

*You make grass grow for the cattle... food to sustain
their strength* (Ps 104:14). He feeds people 'with the
abundance of his house' like honoured guests.

104:10You make springs break out in the wadis,
so that water from them flows between the hills.
11The wild beasts all drink from them,
the wild donkeys quench their thirst.

You let people to drink *from the stream of your delights*. Humans and animals see the sun's light. Only
humans are lit by an inner light: 'Your light makes us see
the light.' Coming out into the light is to be born; seeing
the light is living. But a divine light shines on our human
lives. Being human means opening up to the fullness of
light. As we are surrounded by air and take air into our
lungs, we are also enveloped and bathed in divine light,
which pierces to the marrow of our being. Like swimming
in an ocean where the water supports us and drenches us
and enters through our skin, so is this immortal light.
Indeed, Lord, *your unfailing love reaches to the heavens, your faithfulness to the skies*. We need cosmic di-

mensions to ponder God's greatness. Your unfailing love reaches the farthest galaxies, your faithfulness to the remotest stars. Let us now re-read part of the psalm:

> [5]LORD, your unfailing love reaches to the heavens,
> your faithfulness to the skies.
> [6]Your righteousness is like the lofty mountains,
> your justice like the great deep;
> LORD, who save man and beast,
> [7]how precious is your unfailing love!
> Frail mortals seek refuge in the shadow of your
>   wings.
> [8]They are filled with the bounty of your house,
> and you give them to drink from the stream of your
>   delights.
> [9]For with you is the fountain of life
> and by your light we are enlightened.

Psalm 37
Working and praying
for justice

Half way through the psalm the psalmist declares his age: *I have been young and now I have grown old.* With the weight of this experience he wishes to instruct us: *Never have I seen the righteous forsaken.* We are reluctant to believe him. What authority has an old man who says such things? The rest of the psalm largely disproves this statement. Unless we take the word 'forsaken' to mean something else. Job and Ecclesiastes think otherwise for they have often seen the triumph of injustice, the suffering and abandonment of the innocent. Can such contradictions be reconciled? The old man speaking in this psalm has a profound sense of justice, but also distrusts the violence of oppressors. Because he loves justice and believes in it he hopes for its final victory. This psalmist is definitely on the side of the neglected and oppressed. He has an ideal vision, according to which Joshua, by God's command and by lot, made a fair division of the land, so that each family would have something to live on. He believes that an inner dynamism is pressing towards the attainment or re-attainment of this ideal, a dynamism in which God is at work. He does not preach resignation, but hope. In the face of violence he teaches solidarity and generosity.

If we still find it difficult to enter into the optimistic spirit of the psalm, we may recall that one of its verses is taken up in the third beatitude in Matthew: *The long-suffering shall possess land* (in the old translation: *the meek shall possess the earth*). This verse is repeated with variations five times in the psalm:

> [9]They who hope in the LORD will possess land.
> [11]But the humble will possess land and enjoy untold
>   prosperity.
> [22]Those whom the LORD has blessed will possess land.
> [29]The righteous will possess land.
> [34]He will raise you to be master of land.

Other beatitudes have a verbal or thematic antecedent in this psalm.

The first is *Blessed are the poor*. The psalm knows the oppression of the poor and also their blessedness:

> [14]They have drawn their swords and strung their
>   bows to lay low the oppressed and poor...
> [16]Better is the little which the righteous person hasthan
>   all the wealth of the wicked.

The fourth beatitude is for those who *hunger and thirst for justice*. This is the feeling that pervades the whole psalm and springs from faith in divine justice:

> [5]The LORD will act:
> [6]He will make your righteousness shine clear as the
>   day
> and the justice of your cause like the brightness of
>   noon.
>
> [28]The LORD is a lover of justice
> and will not forsake his loyal servants.

The fifth beatitude is for those who *give help* (the merciful).

The psalm says:

[21]The righteous give generously.
[26]Day in, day out, such a one lends generously.

The seventh beatitude is for the *peacemakers*, a virtue which the psalm preaches against the temptation to violence:

[7]Do not envy those who gain their ends,
or be vexed at their success.
[8]Be angry no more, have done with wrath;
do not be vexed: that leads to evil.

This logically entails suffering persecutions for being innocent and for justice to other innocent people.

Lord, as the years pass do not let me become accustomed or resign myself to injustice. Let me not accept it as an irremediable fatality; but do not let me become exasperated at evil doers or envy wrongdoers. If I cannot work directly for justice, let me at least pray for it saying: Let your kingdom of justice come. Give me your love for justice. *I was young and now I am old, do not abandon me. I know the Lord watches over the upright all their days and their inheritance will last for ever.*

Psalm 38
The trials of Job

I do not feel able to comment on this psalm because I am not in the same situation as the psalmist and I must respect the suffering of others. When Job's friends came to visit him and

> 'when they saw him from a distance, they did not recognise him; they wept aloud, tore their cloaks, and tossed dust into the air over their heads. For seven days and seven nights they sat beside him on the ground, and none of them spoke a word to him, for they saw that his suffering was very great' (Job 2).

They express their friendship, respect and sympathy chiefly by silence. They let him speak and unburden himself, listen to his justifiable complaints and keep him company. It is true that there are old people who enjoy complaining, who boast of their sufferings, because they can no longer boast about anything else. They have a list of their symptoms and of the different pills they are taking. Others who used to be strong and now find their strength going, give way to suffering. Eliphaz, Job's friend, reproaches him as a friend:

4:3Think how you once encouraged many,
how you braced feeble arms,
4how a word from you upheld those who stumbled
and put strength into failing knees.
5But now adversity comes on you, and you are impatient;
it touches you and you are dismayed.

65

And Job replies:

> 6:14Devotion is due from his friends to one who
> despairs and loses faith in the Almighty.

Later on he prays:

> 19:21Pity me, have pity on me,
> you that are my friends,
> for the hand of God has touched me.

For who is more our friend than God, even though it may appear that he has hurt us and is angry with us? Even though he does not intervene physically, Jesus Christ can hear us with compassion:

> Ours is not a high priest unable to sympathise with our weaknesses, but one who has been tested in every way as we are, only without sinning (Heb 4:15).

The psalmist in this psalm, as in many others, relates his suffering to his sins. Even if we do not accept such a mechanical correspondence, it is right to recognise a connection in general. At any rate we can accept our sufferings as a penance and expiation for our sins. Having said this more by way of introduction than commentary, it is good to pray the psalm without interference:

> 1LORD, do not rebuke me in anger
> or punish me in your wrath.
> 2For your arrows have rained down on me
> and your hand on me has been heavy.
> 3Your indignation has left no part of my body
> unscathed;

66

because of my sin there is no health in my whole
    frame.
⁴For my iniquities tower above my head;
they are a heavier load than I can bear.
⁵My wounds fester and stink
because of my folly.
⁶I am bowed down and utterly prostrate.
All day long I go about as if in mourning.
⁷For my loins burn with fever,
and there is no wholesome flesh in me.
⁸Faint and badly crushed
I groan aloud in anguish of heart.
⁹All my longing lies open before you, LORD,
and my sighing is no secret to you.
¹⁰My heart throbs, my strength is spent,
and the light has faded from my eyes.
¹¹My friends and companions shun me in my
    sickness
and my kinsfolk keep far off.
¹²Those who seek my life set their traps,
those who mean to injure me threaten my
    destruction;
they plot all day long.
¹³But I am like a deaf man, hearing nothing,
like a dumb man who cannot open his mouth.
¹⁴I behave like one who does not hear,
whose tongue offers no defence.
¹⁵On you, LORD, I fix my hope;
you, LORD my God, will answer.
¹⁶I said: 'Let them never rejoice over me
who exult when my foot slips.'
¹⁷I am on the brink of disaster,
and pain is constantly with me.
¹⁸I make no secret of my iniquity;
I am troubled because of my sin.

¹⁹But many are my enemies, all without cause,
and numerous are those who hate me without
    reason,
²⁰who repay good with evil,
opposing me because my purpose is good.
²¹But, LORD, do not forsake me;
my God, be not far aloof from me.
²²LORD my deliverer,
hasten to my aid.

Psalm 41
Helping the helpless

We can read this psalm as a continuation and comple-
ment to Psalm 38. Here the psalmist concentrates on the
indifference and hostility he is subjected to. This is a
theme we have already met and which recurs here with
some splendid descriptive touches:

6His case is desperate, my enemies say;
when will he die and his name perish?
6All who visit me speak from hearts devoid of
   sincerity;
they are keen to gather bad news
and go out to spread it abroad.
7All who hate me whisper together about me,
imputing the worst to me:
8An evil spell is cast on him, they say;
he is laid on his bed, and will never rise again.
9Even the friend whom I trusted, who ate at my
   table,
exults over my misfortune.

Here we have plots by rivals or possible successors.
Often remarks by friends and acquaintances that *our case
is desperate* are not ill-meant. They can also be expressing sympathy or resignation. But rivals are ill-meaning,
or so the sufferer imagines. His first request is for health
and mingled in it is the desire for vengeance: Do they
think I am dead and gone? Well, they'll see. He tries to
make God the collaborator or accomplice in his desire to
get his own back.

[11]LORD, be gracious and restore me
that I may repay them in full.

I think a Christian would amend this prayer, because
what our rivals deserve more than anything is sympathy
and understanding. This would be the best way to reproach
them, so that they learn a lesson and do not repeat their
behaviour.

Now let us turn to the beginning of the psalm. What
must we do to gain health? Almost to *deserve* it. The psalm
begins with a blessing (it is the third time we have come
across this; the previous psalms were Psalms 1 and 32).

[1]Happy is anyone who has a concern for the
     helpless!
The LORD WILL save him in time of trouble;
[2]The LORD protects him and gives him life,
making him secure in the land.
The LORD NEVER leaves him to the will of his
     enemies.
[3]On his sick-bed he nurses him,
transforming his every illness into health.

Taking care of the helpless who cannot help themselves accumulates merits for when we ourselves are
struck. This would be a blessing for doctors and nurses.
But not only for them because there are helpless people
in many fields. We can rise directly to God, who rewards
good actions, or we can look at the human process,
through which God discreetly acts. Those who *take care
of the helpless* sow gratitude in those who receive their
care, and one day this gratitude will be translated into
action. Furthermore they spread a spirit of solidarity,
which will bear fruit in perhaps unexpected form. Those
who take care of the helpless are creating or broadening

a sphere of human solidarity in which they are involved, today as givers, but one day as receivers. This is God's way miracles are for extraordinary occasions.

Now let us jump to the end of the psalm, which is an act of trust:

[12]But I am upheld by you because of my innocence; you keep me for ever in your presence.

For the Old Testament psalmist the two are equivalent. Without health he will not be in God's presence, because while he is alive he cannot go into the temple and when he is dead he does not belong to God. For a Christian the two things do not necessarily coincide; they admit of variations. Preserve my health until the day when I am to move into your presence. This means asking for a quick death without a long illness or decrepitude. Preserve my mental health so that I may know I am in God's presence and my physical health so that I can present myself before God in liturgical services. Preserve my health now and assure me that in the beyond I will be in your presence. For a Christian the most important thing is the second part of the prayer, because only in God's house can we say with full truth: *you keep me for ever in your presence.*

Psalms 42-43
The pain of God's absence

This psalm – a single poem with a chorus – is the great prayer of feeling God's absence. We can distinguish two kinds of absence. The first is the absence of many who are absent from our environment and our mind, so that we can concentrate on those who are present and important to us. This is negative absence: we do not miss these people. Secondly we have the absence of something or someone we miss. We can call this feeling nostalgia. Absence is a minus sign with respect to a whole: 18 can be a whole or it can be 20 minus 2. So, when we lack something we count on, 'we miss it', we feel its absence. Do we count on God? This psalm sings God's absence, nostalgia for God.

The paradox is that in our minds, when we feel someone's absence, we make them spiritually present: absence felt is a form of presence. Nostalgia becomes company. This is even more so with God. The psalmist is far from home, the temple, perhaps in exile and he feels God's absence like overpowering thirst:

[1]As a hind longs for the running streams,
so I long for you, my God.
[2]I thirst for God, the living God.

Foreigners who worship other gods who are present in their houses of worship, in images, rub in the wound of God's absence:

³Tears are my food day and night,
while all day long people ask me,
Where is your God?
¹¹My enemies taunt me with crushing insults:
the whole day long they ask, Where is your God?

Nostalgia can be for the past or the future. In the psalm the psalmist longs for a future which will be a return to the past or the continuation of an interrupted rhythm:

⁴As I pour out my soul in distress, I call to mind
how I marched in the ranks of the great to God's
    house,
among exultant shouts of praise,
the clamour of pilgrims.

The future will be God's presence: *when shall I come to appear in your presence?* And then fulfilment will come:

⁴³:³Send out your light and your truth
to be my guide;
let them lead me to your holy hill,
to your dwelling place.
⁴Then I shall come to the altar of God,
the God of my joy and delight,
and praise you with the lyre,
God, my God.

The restoration of the past and the service in the temple will put an end to the evil of absence.

On our lips the psalm is symbolic, with a change of direction. Our nostalgia is not just for the past, although it may incorporate elements of the past, times or moments when we felt God very close, and which awaken a new longing for him. But our actual appointment with God is not in the past, in an innocent childhood or fervent youth. Our appointment with God is in the future. The temple is the symbol of God's dwelling, the liturgy an image of active joy. *When shall I come to appear in your presence?* This means seeing God face to face. While I am still absent and on the way, may God escort me, *give me your light and your truth to be my guide; let them lead me to your dwelling place.*

There is a tension in our relationship with God. If we long for God, this is because he is already present to arouse this desire. If we long for God, it is because he is still absent and we miss him. Absent and present: absence felt is a form of presence. It cannot be otherwise. Let us not think we can count on God and find him when we decide to, as if we could make him do as we please. A God available like that would not be God, my God. If I think I can possess him when I say so, he is no longer God, because I imagine him as manipulable. We should not think that when we open the Bible we will find God automatically present, or when we go to church or take communion. If we think like this, it will be better for God to withdraw so that we painfully feel his absence in his actions.

Elijah was familiar with God, he lived in his presence. One day when he was fleeing from Jezebel, he went on a pilgrimage to Mount Horeb, where the covenant was made through Moses' mediation. God had invited Moses to go into a cave because *the Lord is going to pass by.* Elijah knew the rules for God's appearing, he knew the classic elements of theophany, God's self-manifesting. When he felt a stormy wind, he thought: here is the Lord. *But the Lord was not in the wind.* Then came an earthquake, the earth trembling when it feels the Lord's presence and Elijah thought this was it: here comes the Lord. *But the Lord was not in the earthquake*. Then came a fire, the supreme element of the divinity. Here now the Lord is coming. *But the Lord was not in the fire*. Then came a soft breeze and *Elijah covered his face before the Lord*. Elijah first had to feel God's absence where he expected to find him, in order to be able to receive the new revelation in a *soft breeze*. For his part, Moses, at the height of his familiarity with God, could only see, from the cleft of the rock, God retreating, *his back*.

In this life God always communicates his presence mingled with absence. He regulates the dose in order to calm us sometimes and excite us at other times. He sends us as escorts *his light and his truth*. If he is distant we seek his cooling streams to quench our thirst. If he is close we feel *all your waves, all your breakers sweep over me*. With this alternating absence and presence we repeat the psalm's chorus:

> ⁶How deep I am sunk in misery,
> groaning in my distress!
> I shall wait for God; I shall yet praise him,
> my deliverer, my God.

No poet has succeeded in expressing the pain of absence and longing for God like St John of the Cross in his *Canticle*. It seems as if the Lord's light and truth had inspired these verses and remained in them to lead the reader *to his dwelling-place*. I think that after the psalm, in order to finish our meditation, we can read a few verses of the *Canticle* (or the whole poem if the reader has it to hand):

> Where have you hidden,
> my love, and left me to moan?

You fled like the deer,
you wounded me here.
I cried after you but you were gone.

Oh, who can heal me?
Why can't I have you altogether?
Don't send another
messenger
who will not tell me what I want to hear.

Reveal your presence
and let me die of seeing you and your grace.
My love is an agony
which will not go away
unless it has your presence and your face.

Psalm 44
The suffering Church

Today we are not going to complain about our pains, but we are going to weep for the Church. Our Church which at certain times and places has been triumphant and in others persecuted. The Church in faithful union with its Lord, for whom it suffers persecution. The Church not just as one more body among civil societies, but as the bride of Jesus Christ and bearer of his values. In this sense it is possible for some baptised members of the Church to turn against her or against her values and in fact associate with her enemies. We can sing of this shared pain in the words of the psalm, as long as we read it with a key and translate its images.

Using the key, verses 2-9 can represent the beginning, the establishment and spread of the Church, in the early centuries through the Mediterranean and later in its missionary expansion in various countries. The military images represent her victory over resistance and aggression. A convincing victory involving the shedding of her own blood, not that of others.

Her sword is the word of God. Her enemy is the rival power opposed to the Gospel, which may wear different masks: political, economic, military, social, sexual, doctrinal. Victories of which the Church does not boast because they are not hers, but her Lord's, 'because God has always been our pride.' The victories are the conversion of Paul and of Rome, the faithfulness of the martyrs and the teaching of the holy Fathers, the works of charity and efforts for peace. None of this justifies triumphalism, because it must all be attributed to the Lord. Let us try to read some verses from the beginning of the psalm with this key. If we manage it, we can go on. If we cannot manage it, it will be difficult for us to appropriate the psalm and it will remain immovably anchored in the past, as a simple historical record:

> [3]It was not our fathers' swords that won them the
>   land,
> nor did their strong arm give them victory,
> but your right hand and your arm and the light of
>   your presence;
> such was your favour to them.
> [4]God, you are my king;
> command victory for Jacob.
> [5]By your help we shall throw back our enemies,
> in your name we shall trample down our assailants.
> [6]My trust is not in my bow,
> nor will my victory be won by my sword;
> [7]for you deliver us from our foes,
> you put to confusion those hostile to us.
> [8]In God have we gloried all day long
> and we shall praise your name for ever.

Let us now look back at past ages of persecution, open or hidden. The Church has been persecuted in various countries. Today there are still countries where the Church is persecuted. Because we must remember that the Church consists of its members and *what you did to the least of these my brothers you did to me*: denying help and also torturing and killing. Let us also recall what we have said about Christian values of which the Church is the bearer, because this can also bring persecution. Maybe persecution and killings, maybe mockery and dishonour. We can try a general approach or fix on a particular epoch or place we know best. Let us try our key again with some verses from the second part of the psalm:

> ^{10}You have forced us to retreat before the foe,
> and our enemies have plundered us at will.
> ^{11}You have given us up to be slaughtered like sheep
> and scattered us among the nations.
> ^{12}You sold your people for next to nothing
> and had no profit from the sale.
> ^{13}You have exposed us to the contempt of our
>   neighbours,
> to the gibes and mockery of those about us.

It is a serious matter that the cause of all these ills is God himself, to whom the Church professes fidelity. She reproaches him with complaints full of faith. She knows and confesses that her Lord controls all events and times. It is not a triumph of the enemy power:

> I feared I should be provoked by their foes,
> that their enemies would take the credit,
> saying, 'It was not the LORD
> but we who got the upper hand.'
> They are a nation devoid of good counsel,
> that lacks all understanding (Deut 32:27-28).

(These are verses of the so-called Song of Moses). The Church also complains because she had not deserved to be treated so badly. It is a reasonable and trusting complaint, because the Lord is not despotic or arbitrary. How can his change of attitude and behaviour be explained? Let us continue reading with our key, remembering that even though there are infidelities within the Church, the Christian people as a whole remains faithful to its Lord:

¹⁷Though all this has befallen us, we do not forget
    you,
and have not been false to your covenant;
¹⁸our hearts have not been unfaithful
nor have our feet strayed from your path.
²⁰Had we forgotten the name of our God
and spread our hands in prayer to alien gods,
²¹would not God have found out,
for he knows the secrets of the heart?

As a result, whatever the Church suffers is not through
her fault but for the sake of her Lord:

²²For your sake we are being done to death all day
    long,
treated like sheep for slaughter.

So God's honour is involved and God cannot keep out
of it. With this vigorous conviction we end the psalm
crying:

²³Rouse yourself, LORD; why do you sleep?
Awake! Do not reject us for ever.
²⁶Arise and come to our aid;
for your love's sake deliver us.

Note: This way of praying and meditating with a key
is traditional and legitimate and incorporated into the
liturgy. If we find it difficult or strange, it means we need
practice.

Psalm 45
Let's go to a wedding

Today we are invited to a wedding. We must put on our best clothes for the ceremony. If we remain in the Old Testament we find it is the wedding of a Jewish king with a foreign royal princess. If we translate the psalm into the context of the New Testament, we are talking about the wedding of the Church and the Messiah, in the language of Revelation, the wedding of the Lamb and the new Jerusalem. The Christian reading of this psalm is so traditional and common that it is difficult to translate it back to the kingdom of Judah before the exile. The kings could have various wives and concubines, which made international relations easier. Even with monogamy, royal marriages have played an important political role.

In the royal wedding in the psalm, love rules: *The king has desired your beauty*. The chamberlain is sent to the ceremony of inviting the bride (who has already accepted before the ritual):

> [10]Listen my daughter, hear my words and consider
> them:
> forget your own people and your father's house;
> [11]The king has desired your beauty;
> do him obeisance, for he is your Lord.

Genesis says *the man shall leave father and mother to join with his wife*. In the psalm it is the bride who has to leave her father's house to marry the king. Royal weddings still have a fairy tale aura about them which attract the public.

When you are meditating on this psalm, if you have been married, remember your wedding day. If you have not been married, think of weddings in your family or among your friends.

Who is the *bridegroom* in the psalm? A fine young man, *you surpass all others in beauty*. He speaks with charm: *gracious words flow from your lips*. The Song of Songs puts it more effusively:

> [1:2]Your love is more fragrant than wine,
> [3]fragrant is the scent of your anointing oils,
> your name is like those oils poured out;
> that is why maidens love you.
> [4]Take me with you, let us make haste;
> bring me into your chamber, O king.

As well as these natural qualities, he has kingly ones: he is brave in war, just in peace. Sword, sceptre and throne as his emblems. The sword is the emblem of war *for truth and justice*; the sceptre is *a sceptre of equity*; his throne is the emblem of the house of David: *God has enthroned you for all eternity*. Sword to defend the right, sceptre to administer justice, throne to perpetuate the dynasty. It is not difficult to apply these to Jesus Christ. He was beautiful among men, he spoke wonderfully, *no one spoke like him* (Jn 7:26). He fights for the rights of the oppressed and establishes a reign of justice. He sits on an eternal throne at God's right hand.

Standing beside the king there is another person: *the queen mother*, in accordance with the royal custom of Judah. The mother of the king or the prince who is heir to the throne can bear the title of queen. In the Song of Songs we read:

3:11Come out, maidens of Jerusalem;
you maidens of Zion, welcome King Solomon,
wearing the crown which his mother placed on his
    head
on his wedding day, his day of joy.

In Revelation chapter 12 the mother is probably the Synagogue, or the Jewish community, from whom the Messiah was born. It is also the Church, which gives birth to the members of Christ's body. And according to long tradition, it is Mary, the mother of the bridegroom, the Messiah.

Who is the *bride*? A foreign princess, who has been preferred and chosen from among others for her beauty. The strongest argument for her to accept is the young king's love: *the king has desired your beauty*. Added to this there are signal advantages:

12The city of Tyre will court your favour with gifts,
and the richest of peoples with jewels set in gold.

At that time Tyre was a great trading capital. In the New Testament context the princess is the Church of the pagans, whom the Son of God loves and marries. The most important thing we can say about the Church is that she is the Messiah's bride, united in love and fertile. This could be the first chapter of a biblical ecclesiology. In John's gospel the Baptist's last words are:

3:29It is the bridegroom who marries the bride. The bridegroom's friend, who stands by and listens to him, is overjoyed at hearing the bridegroom's voice. This is my joy and now it is complete. He must grow greater and I must become less.

Growing greater, increasing, refers to fertility: *increase and multiply*. This is the final theme in Psalm 45:

> [16]You will have sons to succeed your fathers,
> and you will make them princes throughout the
>   land.

The Messiah's wedding with the Church will be fertile. There will be children, who will be God's children. The Church can be efficient through organisation but it can only be fruitful through love and union with the Messiah.

We are invited by the psalm to the Messiah's wedding with the Church. Let us celebrate it with joy, as we read in Revelation (19:6-7):

> Hallelujah! The Lord our God, sovereign over all, has entered on his reign! Let us rejoice and shout for joy and pay homage to him, for the wedding day of the Lamb has come! His bride has made herself ready, and she has been given fine linen, shining and clean to wear... Happy are those who are invited to the wedding banquet of the Lamb!

Psalm 47
Drawing nearer to God

A verse of this psalm gives us the theme of our present meditation:

> ⁵To the shout of triumph God has gone up,
> the LORD has gone up at the sound of the horn.

The theme is the ascension. Some writers think there was a procession carrying the ark, the sign of the Lord's presence, going up the temple hill to deposit it in the alcove of the sanctuary (the holy of holies). This would be a dramatic way of representing Yahweh's taking possession of universal power.

Christian tradition has unanimously applied this psalm to Jesus Christ's ascension into heaven, to sit on the throne of universal power. Thus the psalm becomes a poetic version of the story told by Luke at the beginning of the Acts of the Apostles. Some of the psalm's expressions correspond perfectly with this reading, if we apply the traditional title of Lord to Christ:

> ⁵To the shout of triumph the LORD has gone up,
> the LORD has gone up at the sound of the horn.
> ⁷The LORD is King of all the earth;
> sing psalms with all your skill.
> ⁸Seated on his holy throne,
> the LORD reigns over the nations.
> ⁹The princes of the nations assemble
> with the people of the God of Abraham;

for the mighty ones of earth belong to the Lord
and he is exalted on high.

The triumph of Our Lord can be the object of our joyful and glorious meditation. It is the triumph of a member of the human family, our eldest brother. Through him and in him part of the creation ascends to glory. This is the high point for mountains, stars, galaxies. This moment is the climax of millions of cosmic years. As if to say: from the big bang to the ascension of Christ. When Jesus Christ ascends, a new heaven and a new earth are created. A new heaven for the new guest and human Lord that inhabits it; a new earth because it has been filled with his glory. *Clapping, shouts of joy, music are the accompaniment of this ascension.*

Now let us pass in silence to the second point of our meditation, the application to ourselves. We have to go back further.

That is why scripture says:
He ascended into the heights;
he took captives into captivity;
he gave gifts to men.

Now the word 'ascended' implies that he also descended to the lowest level, down to the very earth. He who descended is none other than he who ascended far above all heavens, so that he might fill the universe. (Eph 4:8-10)

It is like running downhill very fast to give a great leap. Or racing downhill in order to go faster up the other side. Christ's ascension is the second half of the parabola. He comes down from heaven, he goes down into his passion and death and from there he ascends. Thus he defines the parabola of all Christian ascension.

Elijah prefigured him in a way. One day the great prophet went up Mount Horeb to meet God (1 Kings 19). From there he was to go down to continue his work and assure the succession. But when the time came he changed direction. Accompanied by Elisha he went down to Jericho, to Jordan. He crossed the river and on the other side he was taken up in a chariot of fire (2 Kings 2). Going down in order to go up. Moses also went down to the plains of Moab before going up to Fasga, whence he contemplated the vision of the promised land which was denied to him. And there he died.

Is old age a descent or an ascent? Sometimes old people are honoured, and their merits finally recognised. When a colleague retires he is given a party in honour and sadness. (Some are only honoured after their death.) It is true that as a whole old age is a slow or rapid decline, a slipping down with nothing to hold onto. But it is going down in order to go up, because we are approaching the great leap. As this will be our final and decisive ascent, we can anticipate its upward movement and transform our inevitable decline into an ascent. In Luke's gospel the ascension begins when Jesus faces the future and begins to go up to Jerusalem (Lk 9), towards the cross, towards heaven. In a moving circular or spherical cosmos what is going down and what is going up? What appears to be going down may really be a movement upwards. Do we fall to the bottom or are we taken up to the top? Much depends on the position we take. Even in our modest planetary and solar world, what we think of as going up, is going down in the antipodes. It is rather like this in the world of the spirit. We try to change position or point of view. The whirlwind took Elijah up, it overcame the force of gravity. Spirits are subject to an upward force of gravity, towards God (or is God in the abyss?) As a body is released from ties restraining it, it is drawn by the force of gravity and its speed accelerates. As our spirit draws nearer to God, its speed increases. You are on the eve of your ascension, it has already begun: *clap your hands, acclaim God with shouts of joy, praise him with psalms, sing psalms with all your skill*: the Lord reigns and you with him.

Psalm 49
Freedom from mortality

Today the teacher is solemn, even severe. He is not going to say a prayer but give a teaching. It is for us to meditate upon it. He says he will play the lyre, but only to accompany his song. I think it will be a sad melody, in a minor key. The teacher is asking a lot, he asks *all nations, all the inhabitants of the world, both high and low, rich and poor* to listen. He is not boasting but merely convinced of the universal value of his teaching. Today he is not speaking about the history of a people, even though it is chosen, but of the human condition. He speaks of every human being and expects all to listen:

[1]Hear this, all you peoples;
listen all you inhabitants of the world,
[2]both high and low,
rich and poor,
[3]for the words I have to speak are wise;
my thoughts provide understanding.
[4]I listen with care to the parable
and interpret a mystery to the music of the lyre.

He is going to expound a proverb or parable or comparison or enigma or puzzle:

[20]for human beings like oxen are short-lived;
they are like beasts whose lives are cut short.

Biologically a human being is like an animal: mortal.

There are insects that only live a few hours, tortoises live more than a hundred and fifty years. A cat can live to twenty, a dog to thirty-five. What about humans? According to Psalm 90, the average is seventy years and if you are robust, eighty. The psalmist of Psalm 49 is not interested in numbers but in the fact. If life ends, the age difference does not count for much. Other differences do not matter either. He will mention riches and wisdom. But do we need a sermon to be convinced? The teacher particularly censors the satisfaction that accumulated riches can bring, as if they were life's meaning and security.

> [6]Trusting in their wealth
> and boasting of their great riches?

It is a frequent teaching that we should not trust in riches but in God.

> This is the man, they say, who would not make God
>   his refuge,
> but trusted in his great wealth, and took refuge in
>   his riches (Ps 52:9).

> Let not the wealthy boast of their wealth (Jer 9: 23).

> Whoever relies on his wealth is riding for a fall (Prov
> 11:28).

Wealth does not assure life. The teacher says that even with great wealth:

> [7]No one can ever ransom himself,
> nor pay God the price for his release;
> [8]the ransom would be too high,

for ever beyond his power to pay,
⁹the ransom that would let him live on for ever
and not see death's pit.

You can pay a ransom to recover some good, e.g. freedom, to commute a penalty, including the death penalty. But the ransom to obtain immortality is too high to pay. Wealth can keep away inconveniences, improve and lengthen life a little, but it cannot buy immortality. When Proverbs 13:8 says: *The rich man pays a ransom for his life*, this means a few more years of life. So the teacher adds the macabre vision of people like a flock led by a macabre shepherd:

¹³Such is the fate of the foolish
and of those after them who approve their words.
¹⁴Like sheep they head for Sheol;
with Death as their shepherd,
they go straight down to the grave.
Their bodies, stripped of all honour, waste away in
    Sheol.

The dead are a great faceless human flock. Death is their shepherd. What does he graze them on? Where does he lead them?

The teacher concentrates mostly on the rich, but he also briefly has something to say about the wise, the teachers, those of his own profession. So he is preaching to himself as well and cannot be accused of partiality:

¹⁰For we see that the wise die,
as the stupid and senseless all perish.

There are teachers who are rich in knowledge, loaded with wisdom. They also are tempted to feel self-satisfied with their accumulated knowledge. Of them the author can say, *at his death he can take nothing*. All that remains will be what they have given, what they have communicated to others. Thus the comparison. Has it taught us anything new? Perhaps its novelty lies in its tone and way of teaching. So where is the enigma? It arises in contrast to the previous vision. Does the universal law admit of any exceptions? The teacher replies:

[15]But God will ransom my life
and take me from the power of Sheol.

Sheol means death. His hands seek us when we are born and clasp us when we die. Is there anything stronger? Isaiah says (49:24):

Can the spoil be snatched from the strong man,
or a captive liberated from the ruthless?

God is stronger than Sheol: he frees, and snatches. Does this explain the enigma? The author uses the Hebrew verb *pth*, which means open, resolve. In the Old Testament context the affirmation in verse 16 is the great enigma and we have to seek its solution in the New Testament.

No one can ever ransom himself, nor pay God the price for his release. But someone gave his life as a ransom for many (Mt 20:28). We do not trust in piled up wealth or in accumulated knowledge. We trust that, through Jesus Christ and with him God will take us and carry us to himself. Now let us read a page from Paul, with brief commentaries as we go along, in order to help our meditation. The passage is from Romans chapter 8:

[19]Humanity is waiting with eager expectation for God's children to be revealed.

Humanity is a probable translation for *ktisis* (corresponding to the Aramaic *beri' a*) and contrasted with 'us Christians' in verse 23. Being children of God means receiving immortality, because a child of God cannot end up as a slave to death. This is shown as follows:

[20]For it was made subject to frustration, not of its own choice but by the will of him who subjected it, yet with the hope [21]that humanity itself is to be freed from the shackles of mortality and is to enter upon the glorious liberty of the children of God.

'Frustration' or vanity, the *mataiotes* of Ecclesiastes, 'vanity of vanities, all is vanity', because it ends in death. In Psalm 39: *A human being is but a puff of wind*, which sounds in Hebrew like 'every Adam is Abel'. Being mortal is a frustration for a conscious being wanting to liberate itself from the curse of death but who cannot do so alone.

[22]Up to the present, as we know, the whole humanity in all its parts groans as if in the pangs of childbirth.

The whole of humanity, like a woman in labour, is straining to give birth to the new humanity (cf Rev 12), that is worthy of a higher destiny. The whole of humanity is contrasted with the Christians who are already liberated in part but not totally. With their experience of part fulfilment they long for the whole more consciously:

[23]What is more, we also, to whom the Spirit is given as the firstfruits of the harvest to come, are groaning inwardly while we look forward eagerly to our adoption, our ransom from mortality.[24]It was with this hope that we were saved.

This Spirit is the one who raised Jesus from the dead (8:11). He is the firstfruits we receive as elder children (Christians) or as an anticipation of what is to come. We are still lacking the liberation from mortality, of our body which was surrendered in the death of Jesus Christ.

[24]Now to see something is no longer to hope: why hope for what is already seen? [25]But if we hope for something we do not yet see, then we look forward to it eagerly and with patience.

Verse 11 has already said what we look forward to with patience:

[11]If the Spirit of him who raised Jesus from the dead dwells in you, then the God who raised Christ Jesus from the dead will also give new life to your mortal bodies through his indwelling Spirit.

Psalm 55
A prayer for peace

I am going to concentrate on one verse of this dramatic psalm:

[17] Evening and morning and at noonday
I make my complaint and groan.
[18] He will hear my cry and deliver me
and give me peace.

We could try another translation and take the word 'peace' adverbially: deliver me peacefully, that is, without violence, gently. The end result does not change that much: this is an intense plea for the coming of peace and serenity through God's action. We nearly all want peace, but in 'the third age' this desire becomes stronger. I heard an old lady who had lived through the last war and lost her husband in it say that if another war broke out she would commit suicide. Perhaps she wouldn't really. But what she said shows that she did not want to or could not live without peace. Even old people who boast of their military exploits when young, I do not think would like to repeat them now. But apart from war, strictly speaking, haven't all of us had to struggle during our lives? Studies, job, competition, bringing up the family, politics, business... Now that the time for struggle is over, peace is more delicious.

So the psalm makes much of peace because it is peace amid struggle and anarchy. As if by an occupying power, the city is inhabited and overrun by sinister figures:

Crime, Injustice, Calamity, Cruelty, Deceit. The police patrolling the city are called Violence and Discord. In the midst of this situation the psalmist finds peace:

9I have seen Violence and Strife in the city;
10day and night they encircle it, all along its walls;
it is filled with Trouble and Mischief,
11Destruction is rife within it;
its public square is never free from Oppression and
    Deceit.

As if it were a little thing, these times of anarchy and disorder are times when friends betray you:

12It was no enemy that taunted me,
or I should have avoided him;
no foe that treated me with scorn,
or I should have kept out of his way.
13It was you, a man of my own sort,
a comrade, my own dear friend;
14we held pleasant converse together
walking with the throng in the house of God.

It was a friendship bathed in religious feeling, that now has been betrayed. His heart is sore, but the psalmist turns to God and finds peace.

Surrounded in the city by hostile forces, and inwardly suffering, he plans flight. In these circumstances the barren desert would be more hospitable. But his flight is purely imaginary:

6I say: Oh that I had the wings of a dove
to fly away and find rest!
7I would escape far away
to a refuge in the wilderness.

[8]Soon I would find myself a shelter from raging wind and tempest.

The imaginary flight does not remedy anything, because the enemy's voice and his cries of ill will come through the wall of the refuge and assault him.

[3]I am panic-stricken by hostile shouts,
at the shrill clamour of the wicked...
[4]My heart is torn with anguish
and the terrors of death bear down on me.

In spite of everything, he finds peace. The only way out is to turn to God, continually, without allowing himself or God any respite. Until God frees my soul gently, calmly; until he brings me tranquillity. What Jerusalem, the 'city of peace', does not give him, God gives him: peace. In conclusion, let us listen to his recommendation and give our response:

[22]Commit your fortunes to the LORD.
[23]For my part, LORD, I shall put my trust in you.

Psalm 57
A new dawn

There are old people who wake up early and look forward to the dawn. Others like to lie in bed and sleep longer, wishing that the sun would not be so punctual. The psalmist in this psalm is impatient for dawn to come. He wakes up himself and then wakes up his musical instrument. With his music he tries to hurry the dawn, which seems to be delaying (as when we make music to wake a person up, loudly or softly). Once dawn has come he calls upon the sun to shed its light on all the earth. Is this a sun rite? The psalmist is like a new Joshua in reverse. Joshua ordered the sun to hide; the psalmist orders the sun to appear. Or is it a rite to stimulate himself. The music of his lyre does not alter the rhythm of the music of the spheres, the heavenly music.

At least it is not a daily ritual. The psalmist finds himself in a dangerous situation and hopes that help will arrive at sunrise. Like a very sick person who is waiting for essential medicine to arrive by the first post. In imaginative, perhaps hyperbolical language he tells us:

[4]I lie prostrate among lions, man-eaters
whose teeth are spears and arrows,
whose tongues are sharp swords.

I do not suppose we are in such a critical situation. Nevertheless we have learnt to pray and meditate with a key.

The first thing we do will be to refer the text to Christ:

98

this is called the Christological reading or 'allegory' in Patristic and mediaeval exegesis. Christ is hidden in the tomb and it is night in the world. Humanity is lying between the wild beasts of hatred and selfishness, between the sharp tongues of deceit and falsehood. It impatiently prays for the coming of the liberator, Christ's resurrection. Impatiently it gets up and rouses itself, plays and sings its best songs, hurries the dawn, calls to the Lord.

[7]My heart is steadfast, God,
my heart is steadfast.
I shall sing and raise a psalm.
[8]Awake, my soul,
awake harp and lyre.
I shall awake at dawn.
[11]God be exalted above the heavens;
let your glory be over all the earth.

Rise again, Lord, to new life. Start the day that will not set and let the light of your glory shine and give light to all peoples. Let it be the light that gives light to all. Love of Christ becomes missionary impatience. Prayer for an Easter morning, on a mountain, making music to greet the royal apparition of the sun.

Now we are going to move to the end of time, to Christ's second coming or parousia. This key the ancients call *anagogia* or ascension, because mentally in contemplation we rise to meet the Lord. The parousia can be thought of at the end of time, for human history, and also can refer to the individual Christian, for whom time is ending and eternity is dawning. With this key the psalm takes on new meaning, related to the previous one. There are old people who want to go on sleeping, even though they are lying among lions. In spite of troubles, they are attached to life and do not want to lose it. They want the sun to delay. It is all very well to feel impatient for Christ's resurrection and the shining of his glory. But not impatience for his second coming, which will snatch me out of this life. On the other hand, we have known old people who are tired of living in hope, others who are serene in feeling they are ripe for the harvest; others who are longing finally to meet the Lord. St John of the Cross sings of his impatience with an intensity that the conventions of the literary form cannot disguise. I only quote part of the poem. I leave the reader to read the whole poem and meditate on it alone:

I live but do not live in me
and hope for life so high
that I die because I do not die.

I no longer live in me
and without God I cannot live;
without him and without myself
what will this living be?
A thousand deaths are done to me
because I await my very life
dying because I do not die.

Absent from you, not with,
what life can I have
but suffering death —
none worse do I see.
I am sorry for me
because I go on being this way,
dying because I do not die.

Following our poet perhaps one day we'll dare to wake to the dawn and sing:

God be exalted above the heavens;
let your glory be over all the earth.

Psalm 62
Trust in God

What are human beings made of? Their body is a system of forces in cohesion, a balanced play of functions. We stay on earth by the force of gravity and because the earth resists. In the sea we sink and we try to prevent this by swimming. In the air we fall and need support. We build walls, buildings, sky-scrapers, using materials that stick together and support them by the force of gravity. So what is our spiritual cohesion? What we are or what we possess? A human being is a possibility that becomes a being, a being that cannot cease to be. Death which is always at hand, although deferred, decay and old age, sickness and mutilation are manifestations of contingency, of a being that does not have consistency in itself. Good and happy experiences happen and are over, they no longer exist and sometimes they are no longer even remembered. The psalm says something similar from another point of view:

⁹The common people are mere empty air,
while people of rank are a sham;
when placed on the scales they rise
all of them lighter than air.

Psalm 39 said that each person is a breath of air. This psalm says that all people together are less than a breath of air, because of their lightness and brevity. So where is their weight?
We look for a wall to lean against, ballast to weigh us

down. But when we are afraid of losing our place or in order to enlarge it we attack our neighbours. Destruction is the great work of selfishness:

>³How long will you assail with your threats,
>all beating against your prey,
>as if he were a leaning wall,
>a toppling fence?

Truth rests on what is, it has the consistency of reality. Truth is a force of gravity towards being. Lies and falsehood have no support in reality. They are an instrument of destruction to supplant what is by what is not, to wreck trust and cohesion among people:

>⁴They aim to topple him from his height.
>They take delight in lying;
>they bless him with their lips
>but curse him in their hearts.

People use riches as ballast. They think that by possessing they can compensate for what they lack in being. Rather than a substantive or noun, the human being is a possessive: compensating for lack of substance by possession. But the lust for possession leads to injustice, either because the goods are insufficient or because those who possess them are not satisfied. Then come oppression, exploitation, robbery:

>¹⁰Put no trust in extortion,
>no false confidence in robbery.

And what if wealth increases not in order to be robbed but to be productive and shared? Then it would be legitimate. Could we then trust in it? The psalm continues:

[10]though wealth increases,
do not set your heart on it.

Perhaps the years have opened our eyes so that we
appreciate the value and real weight of the good things in
life. When we feel heavier, we appreciate lightness. We
see that wealth is a distraction, a weighing down, rather
than a ballast.

So with the psalmist let us seek our support in God.
The only support for contingency is pure infinite being.
The psalmist tells us in these words, preferring language
which is physical rather than metaphysical:

[2]He only is my rock of deliverance,
my strong tower, so that I stand unshaken.
[7]On God my safety and my honour depend,
God who is my rock of refuge and my shelter.

We should note that in Hebrew 'my honour' is *kebodi*,
which etymologically means 'my weight, my gravity.'

[1]For God alone I wait silently;
my deliverance comes from him.
[8]Trust in him at all times, you people;
pour out your hearts before him;
God is our shelter.

Pouring out our hearts before God and resting in him
are two complementary acts. When we pour out our
hearts, we unburden ourselves of all the sorrow and
weight that fill and darken and stifle us. Then feeling
light and free we can rest in God. Because we do not seek
a weight of sorrow as a ballast, but a gentle support that
we find in God.

A past or present support? Let us return to our metaphysical speculation. The Scolastics teach us that contingent being finds its initial support in creation, its present support in conservation, and support for its action in concurrence. That is to say, at every moment of being and doing it is directly supported by infinite being. And what about the future? Here comes the paradox:

[5]For God alone I wait silently,
my hope comes from him.

We rely on the past, goods we have acquired, or merits we have earned. We rely on the present, in our vital force that continues. Do we also rely on the future? We rely on God who made us and preserves us. Do we also rely on the God of our future? This is hope: a hook that hooks onto us before we come into port, the hanging ladder by which we climb up. Not that God has a future, since he is purely present, but our future is in God and we hang on to him, we rely on him:

[5]For God alone I wait silently;
my hope comes from him.

Psalm 63
God in all things

A better music sounded in my senses, said St John of the Cross, and in this psalm once again — as in Psalm 34 — the senses are going to feel and express the draw of the divine music, that music that is more attractive than the sirens' song. The very beginning of the psalm is eager expectation:

> [1]God, you are my God; I seek you eagerly
> with a throat that thirsts for you
> and a body wasted with longing for you,
> like a dry land, parched and devoid of water.

I wake impatiently because when I sleep I am away from you without feeling it. Because you even slip into my sleep to disturb me and wake me up with the intensity of my longing. I wake competing with the dawn, which breaks through the darkness of the horizon so that the sun can appear. And you give me light within, the sweetness of dawn, the brightness of the sun. I wake not because I am dying to get to work or because I have to go on an early journey, or to enjoy the earth's early morning freshness. No; I wake for you, you are my task and my success, my journey and its happy ending. What happiness when our first thought and wish on waking is of God and to discover that he was waiting for us:

> Those who love me I love
> and those who seek me will find me
> says Wisdom inviting (Prov 8:17).

As soon as I wake up I feel thirsty. The weather is dry, perhaps I have been sweating. I am aware that my throat is dry and this reminds me that in a certain sense water is my element. The 'throat' (*nepes*) is also the soul. Physical thirst is nothing compared with thirst for God. For you are my element, inside and out, my God. My throat is thirsty for water, my soul is thirsty for God. As the hind pants for living streams, *like a dry land, parched and devoid of water*. Water is life, the earth's fertility. Lord, what harvest can I bear if you do not water me and drench me? My drooping leaves need watering by you. You are my water. Dreaming of it will not do:

> Like one who is thirsty and dreams that he is drinking but wakes to find himself faint with thirst (Is 29:8).

My soul is longing, fainting for you. Because *flesh is like grass* (Is 40:6). Flesh is weak without your breath. *I seek you eagerly, with a throat that thirsts for you, and a body wasted with longing for you.*

At the other extreme from morning is the night: time to sleep, time to dream. Not yet, Lord, but time to think of you:

> ⁶I call you to mind on my bed
> and meditate on you in the night watches,
> for you have been my help.

During the day, Lord, I have been doing my work, which took all my attention. During the day all sorts of things have happened, without time to ponder them. Night is the time to go over things in my mind, ponder and take things in. But I have one thing above all to remember and meditate on: you, my God. Because all through this day and many other days *you have been my help*. For fifteen hours, almost without my realising it, you have kept me and worked with me, *you have been my help*. So Lord, let me spend a moment concentrating on your presence. The memory of you calms me, meditating on you gives me rest. If anything keeps me awake, it is not my worries but you. My body is wasted with longing for you and lies down on my bed to rest: now it does not distract me. My busy abstracted mind concentrates to think about you. Even though it was full of so many things, it was half empty; only with you does it feel full. I am happy in my bed, where the memory of you reawakens, my bed that shelters my meditation. Before I close my eyes and senses I shall remember what they felt during the day. Eyes:

²With such longing I see you in the sanctuary
and behold your power and glory.

In the temple I see the fine architecture, the use of space, the rows of columns, instant and permanent harmony. In it and beyond it I contemplate you. The forces that hold it up teach me your power. The shining granite, the splendour of the courtyard enhanced by the darkness show me your glory. They show me your power and glory, because *heaven and earth are full of your glory*. My eyes see and my spirit contemplates. All creation is translucent and what shines through is you. *With such longing I see you in the sanctuary and behold your power and glory.*

Taste: In the temple I enjoy with others the sacrificial banquet. As I satisfy my appetite I am your guest at table. You share out the victims' meat and

⁵I am satisfied as with a rich feast

and *he who eats shall feel more hungry* (Eccl 24:21). I enjoy savouring you, because I know : *Taste and see that* the LORD is good (Ps 34:9). Lord, refine my taste, so that I may discover a thousand savours in you and never grow tired of you:

> [5]I am satisfied as with a rich feast
> and there is a shout of praise on my lips.

Touch: I remember when I was a child and held my father's hand and we walked along with unequal steps. I felt the contact of his hand; warm and firm with this hand my father communicated with me. Or if I was tired of walking, perhaps my mother took me in her arms and I breathed against her breasts. Now much more:

> [8]I follow you closely
> and your right hand upholds me.

Oh, to feel contact with God inside and out. His firmness, tenderness, his warmth, his elasticity making me bend. Oh, to be pressed against him, feel his strength and that no one can tear me away. To be in contact with him, waiting for the final embrace of God, like a father and mother:

> [7]I am safe in the shadow of your wings.
> I follow you closely
> and your right hand upholds me.

When the supreme moment comes will it be a restful night, when meditating turns into presence? Will it be a dawn without thirst or fainting? Meanwhile, Lord, awaken my senses and raise them towards you, because:

> [3]Your unfailing love is better than life;
> therefore I shall sing your praises.
> Thus all my life I bless you.

Psalm 65
God's presence in the world

Once, when they told Jesus off for working on the sabbath, he argued back: *My Father goes on working and I work.* Thus he corrected an over-literal interpretation of Genesis chapter 1. In philosophical language we would say that God is above the distinction between work and rest. He transcends these human categories. On another occasion Jesus said in metaphorical language: *My Father is the farmer.* Thus he gave an example of a particular kind of work in accordance with the culture in which he lived. In our culture, could we say that the Father is the worker, the engineer? We can use many images to express some inexpressible aspect of God. Today we are going to look at the agricultural image offered to us by Psalm 65.

God is the farmer, the father of a large family who has to support his children. With love for his family, respect for the earth and its rhythms, he carefully carries out the farmer's various jobs: ploughing, watering, hoeing, tending the young plants, looking after the vines and fruit trees he has planted on hillsides, grass to pasture his stock. As we read the text we should note how detailed it is:

[9]You care for the earth and make it fruitful;
you enrich it greatly,
filling its great channels with rain.
In this way you prepare the earth
and provide grain for its people.

¹⁰You water its furrows, level its ridges,
soften it with showers and bless its growth.
¹¹You crown the year with your good gifts;
places where you have passed drip with plenty;
¹²the open pastures are lush
and the hills wreathed in happiness;
¹³the meadows are clothed with sheep
and the valleys decked with grain,
so that with shouts of joy they break into song.

At the end we see a broad landscape, green with grass, woolly white and the valleys golden with corn.

We are accustomed to thinking of God as a creator, who brings things into being. We are less used to perceiving God as perpetually active in his creation. As if the seventh day brought his tasks to an end and he settled down to perpetual rest. This is the picture Jesus wants to correct: *My Father goes on working*. Philosophers call this the doctrine of divine concurrence. In his contemplation to attain love, St Ignatius proposes a particular point on God's permanent activity. We should frequently exercise this type of contemplation. We should think not only of the harmonious beauty of this fir tree, the leafiness of that beech, but also of their powerful roots, the strength of the sap rising to reach every sprout and leaf and flower and cone and nut. The power that transforms the earth's juices into precise shapes of flowers and fruits which smell and taste. God is active in the condor hovering, the whale ploughing through the ocean, the leaping gazelle. Hadn't you noticed? *You crown the year with good gifts*. He not only starts off but crowns, because he accompanies the whole cycle. *He restrains the roaring of the sea*. But he is also active in the swing of the tides, the waves' swell, the undersea currents. And in the star world and the world of sub-atomic particles. Who can grow tired of contemplating all this? If we have been forced to retire by society or by our own bodies, we can devote ourselves to contemplating this marvellous, multiple and secret activity of God. He also collaborates with our own activity. We can focus our observation inwards or outwards. Just as weight is not inertia but an ever active force of attraction, as light which appears immobile is high-speed energy, God's energy is active. *Heaven and earth are full of your glory* in action.

The Lord is also present in history in an open or secret way:

5Through dread deeds you answer us with victory,
God our deliverer.

True, often what we see is injustice, and God does not seem to understand or care. We see the power of the sense of justice among human beings: work for the common good, dialogue, understanding, collaboration agreement. A moment may come in which a process of justice is precipitated in the world or a region.

They are *portents of justice* in which God acts.

The psalm text introduces God as protagonist. John's gospel calls him my Father. This is a detail that should enrich our meditation. In the psalm we see God working hard. According to St John all God's activity is fatherly and loving. In our contemplation we are astounded by God's prodigious activity and filled with joy by his personal affection:

8The dwellers at the ends of the earth are overawed
   by your signs;
you make the gates of dawn and sunset sing aloud
   in triumph.

East and west, the gates of dawn and sunset, are the two extreme points of the sun's daily journey. Let us take them as symbols. If we identify dawn with birth, which we do not remember, our joy is stored up until we are able to celebrate our birthday. Likewise sunset signifies death. Can this fill us with joy? At least with certain hope.

[5]God our deliverer,
in whom all put their trust
at the ends of the earth and on distant seas.

We are approaching sunset to keep an inevitable appointment. *Every mortal comes to you.* (*'Ad te omnis caro veniet'*, says the Vulgate, quoted in the Liturgy of the Dead.) Let us pray the Father to direct his activity to fill us with joy:

[4]Happy are those whom you choose
and bring near to remain in your courts.
Grant us in abundance the bounty of your house,
of your holy temple.

Psalm 67
The power to bless

Who blesses? God. Who pronounces the blessing calling upon the Lord to bless us? According to Numbers 6:23 the priests descended from Aaron: '*Say this to Aaron and his sons: These are the words with which you are to bless the Israelites.*' According to Genesis 27, the old father gives a blessing before he dies, to establish the legitimate heir. According to Genesis 14, it is for the foreign priest Melchisedech. According to Numbers 23-24 it is Balaam, the sorcerer and soothsayer, under the power of the Lord. In Psalm 67 if a president of the liturgy is speaking, he does so in the name of the whole community, as is shown by the plural:

[1]May God be gracious to us and bless us,
may he cause his face to shine on us.

The blessing has a double content. For the earth, fertility: *the earth has yielded its harvest*. For the nations, just government: *you judge the people with equity and guide the nations of the earth.*

In Genesis 47:7-10 we shall see how Jacob as an old man blesses the great Pharaoh. Perhaps any old person, by virtue of their years, may invoke God's blessing, for the earth's prosperity and for just rulers.

Psalm 71
The gift of old age

This psalm is explicitly an old person's prayer: *Now that I am old and my hair is grey*. The psalmist feels threatened and in grave danger. Experience has taught him to trust in the Lord: *you are my rock and my stronghold*. From his old age he looks back over his whole life and a few salient moments. He goes back to his *birth*, according to Hebrew custom, supposing that birth defines a life's direction:

> [6]On you I have leaned from birth;
> you brought me from my mother's womb.

God controls all of life, including this mysterious phase spent in our mother's womb. At this stage the creature does not know itself but God knows it completely. Only the mother is aware of a presence and God directs the whole process. When others only see a lump, God is forming it. Psalm 139 explains a little more:

> [13]You it was who fashioned my inward parts;
> you knitted me together in my mother's womb.
> [15]My body was no mystery to you,
> when I was formed in secret,
> woven in the depths of the earth.
> [16]Your eyes foresaw my deeds.

The mother of the Maccabees declares her ignorance in 2 Maccabees 7:

[22]You appeared in my womb, I know not how; it was not I who gave you life and breath, nor I who set in order the elements of your being. [23]It was the creator of the universe who designed the beginning of mankind and devised the origin of all.

In biblical times gestation and birth were much more dangerous processes than now. Mother and child were threatened by forces they knew nothing about. When the child arrived safely the parents felt the presence of divine help: *You sustained me*. Psalm 22 also expresses this feeling:

[9]But you are he who brought me from the womb,
who laid me at my mother's breast.
[10]To your care I was entrusted at birth;
from my mother's womb you have been my God.

Jeremiah goes even further back. He was chosen for his mission before he was born or even conceived (Jer 1).

A second important stage of life is *adolescence and youth*, the apprentice years. A large part of our physical development is over whereas our intellectual and spiritual development is just taking off. This is a time when good teachers are of crucial importance.

As he looks back the psalmist realises that he has had a single teacher:

[17]You have taught me from childhood, God.

It has not just been theoretical instruction. God has also taught through life's experiences, his written and spoken word, inner callings, the teachings of those who transmit his messages. Psalm 16:7 confesses:

⁷In the night he imparts wisdom to my inmost
   being.

The psalmist of Psalm 119 begs God to instruct him
more than ten times. In Psalm 94:10 God is given the
title of Teacher.

Thank you, Lord, because from my youth you have
put me in contact with good and great teachers: the
works of St Augustine and St Thomas, so many writings
of our Christian tradition. But thank you even more that
you have taught me through prayer and contemplation,
in spiritual exercises. Thank you for being accessible in
person, by which I have learnt the most important things
in the most effective way. Thank you too because as well
as teaching me you have corrected me and not spared
me. In Proverbs 22 we read:

¹⁵Folly is deep-rooted in the hearts of children;
a good beating will drive it out of them.
⁶Start the child on the right road,
and even in old age he will not leave it.

Many years have passed. What shall I say about
them? The psalmist refers to them as a whole. If we are
appropriating the psalm we can pause a while to remember important moments in our lives. Let us try:

²⁰You made me suffer many grievous hardships.

Physical dangers: illnesses, accidents, operations.
Spiritual dangers: dangerous company, temptations,
deception and bewilderment. But you were *my hope and
my trust*. So:

⁸⁷My mouth will be full of your praises,
I shall tell of your splendour all day long.

Now old age has come. Reaching it is another gift of God's, a prolonged victory of life. Every year of our life is a gift from God, but after seventy, every year is a bonus. We like to go on living, we do not want to give in to old age. But let us not be fussy. Old age is also a gift if God is with us:

9Do not cast me off when old age comes
or forsake me as my strength fails.
18Now that I am old and my hair is grey
do not forsake me, God.

Many old people are abandoned or rejected by their families, because they say they have no room for them. Others are abandoned by colleagues who say they have no time for them. Often our strength abandons us, our senses fail and we are out of touch. We grow tired of reading, we do not follow a conversation. We lose interest in taking part. But you at least, my God, *do not abandon me*. My old age reminds you of all you have done for me. Every birthday reminds you of my birth. After looking after me for seventy years, are you going to abandon me? Psalm 138:

8Your love endures for ever, LORD;
do not abandon what you have made.

Are you tired of me? I am not tired of you. Lord, *now that I am old and my hair is grey, do not forsake me*. Do not forsake me because there is still something left for me to do, perhaps quite a lot:

18Do not forsake me, God,
until I have extolled your strength
to generations yet to come.

For years I have gathered a centuries-old tradition and accumulated experience about God. Now I must pass it on to others, like a torch in a relay. If *all my life I have proclaimed your marvellous works*, I must go on doing so, because I have not finished. *All day long my tongue will tell of your vindicating power.* Your power has no limit:

[18]until I have extolled your strength to generations yet to come [19]your might and vindicating power to highest heaven;
for great are the things you have done. Who is there like you, my God?

Do not forsake me also means do not let hope forsake me, the hope with which I look to the future now at hand, the trust with which I rest in God. Advent prepares us to commemorate the Lord's first coming, giving us hope. Advent also reminds us of the Lord's second coming and confirms us in this hope:

[5]You are my hope, LORD GOD,
my trust since my childhood.
[14]But as for me, I shall wait in continual hope,
I shall praise you again and yet again.

I know that you have not forsaken me up till now and you will not abandon me in my old age. The fact that I can meditate on the songs you inspired proves that you have not forsaken me. In the end you will welcome me. Because if I hope in you, you are waiting for me:

[20]You revive me once more
and lift me again from earth's watery depths.
[21]Restore me to honour,

and comfort me again;
²²then I shall praise you on the harp
for your faithfulness, my God.

There remain many psalms to meditate on. I hope the
ones I have picked out may serve as examples.

Part II

Biblical portraits of old people

Introduction

When a famous person dies, the town puts up a memorial, an author is given a biography. The statue perpetuates a moment in his or her life, a frequent gesture, an attitude that expresses or symbolises what is most characteristic. If the statue is in the middle of a square or an avenue, it is glad to be of bronze or stone and not have to breathe in traffic fumes, which would be like dying a second time. If it is put up in a park, it will look down on children playing, who will unconsciously get used to greatness. (I am thinking of the statue of Columbus in Madrid and Nelson's Column in Trafalgar Square in London). A biography is not exhibited in public but lies quietly on library shelves. Nevertheless, I think it is the best memorial to a person and the best way of keeping them present.

Perhaps we do not think it concerns us, because no one is going to put up a statue to us or write our biography. We are not that important. Perhaps we are not for our fellow human beings, but to God we are. Everyone is important to God, everyone is called to be God's child and heir, to be intimate with God. But God's ways are different. Genesis chapter 2 shows God as a potter or sculptor and quite a few Old Testament texts call him the modeller (Hebrew root *ysr*). The model is not finished, it still lacks the final touch. Job complained to God of his terrible sickness:

$^{10:8}$Your hands shaped and fashioned me;
and will you at once turn and destroy me?

As if God were a capricious sculptor, who has grown tired of his work and decided not to finish it. God is not like this. Even though we suffer sickness like Job, God continues to shape us, even through the sickness, until he gives us the final touch.

I still prefer the image of the biography. Do we write it ourselves or does God write it? A good novelist puts his characters in critical or testing situations and observes how they react. This is how his novel progresses. Likewise God puts us in situations where we have to decide, *to humble and test you and discover whether or not it was in your heart to keep his commandments* (Deut 8:2). Large or small decision by which we form ourselves and show ourselves, because what has not yet been formed cannot show itself. Our biography still has to be finished and who can say whether the last chapter will be the most important one. There is a book of poems by Gerardo Diego called *Unfinished Biography*: a good title for ourselves. If it is for us to write it, we should let God guide our hand. One day, God knows when, we will come to the words THE END, meaning: here begins the second part, the better part.

Now we are going to look at some portraits of old people in the Bible. They had different missions in life and we can learn something from each of them. There are Old and New Testament characters and I shall present them as a frieze, like a series of presidents in a university hall or saints in a church.

(I leave it to a woman writer to write on old female figures in the Bible.)

Simeon
Hope was his daily bread

My first is Simeon and I call him our special patron. Is he Old or New Testament? Both, because they meet in him. 'Old Simeon' has become an almost archetypal figure of the old man for us. As such he is a good gospel model for us. The old man whose name was Simeon.

Simeon lengthened his days because of his desire to live, his need to live. He lived to see the day. This desire was fed within him by the secret voice of the Holy Spirit, who was his particular counsellor. There can be no doubt that the old man Simeon had often recited Psalm 16 and benefited from this verse:

> [7]I shall bless the LORD who has given me counsel:
> in the night he imparts wisdom to my inmost being.

Simeon could be sure on one point:

> [119:99] I have more insight than all my teachers.

He knew that the expected Messiah would arrive during his lifetime. What Simeon was to see with his eyes was the most important thing in Israel's history: *'Truly I tell you: many prophets and saints longed to see what you now see, yet never saw it'* (Mt 13:17). The exact date was fixed by God, but the Spirit had not revealed this detail to Simeon, so that he might live in hope from day to day. If I go to bed tonight without having seen him, this means I have another day to live. Hope was his daily bread, his manna for the journey.

Israel's best people had learnt to turn their faces towards the future, without forgetting the past. It was a profound mental and spiritual conversion that changed the meaning of their lives. In the Hebrew language, the future is behind our back, because we do not know it, the past is in front. By half turning round, the best people in Israel faced the future. Simeon was one of these chosen ones. He just lived through this experience with such intensity that he embodies them all. Simeon is like the old regime, the history of Israel, drawing itself out to greet the arrival of the Messiah. We can quote a verse of Habakkuk to Simeon:

> 2:3There is still a vision for the appointed time.
> It will testify to the destined hour and will not
>   prove false.
> Though it delays, wait for it,
> for it will surely come before too long.

Hope becomes expectation and may turn into impatience. Psalm 130:

> 5I wait for the LORD with longing;
> I put my hope in his word.
> 6My soul waits for the LORD
> more eagerly than watchmen for the morning.
> 7Like those who watch for the morning,
> let Israel look for the LORD.

Did Simeon feel impatience? We can imagine him divided, torn between two feelings. The longer the Messiah delays, the longer he will live. Love of life invites him to hope for delay. But the longing to see the Messiah impels him to want the time to be shorter, even though that means living less long. Impatience for the event or the enjoyment of a long evening. But by now Simeon does not live to enjoy what remains of life. Life has already given him everything it was going to give. He only goes on living in order to keep his appointment.

Simeon lives with the mature serenity of his years and the joy given him by the Holy Spirit in whom he trusts. The scriptures speak in general of the coming of the Messiah: the Spirit has read him the classic texts giving them a personal application. In his intimacy with the Spirit Simeon also represents the best of Israel. What is said in Amos 3:7 goes for him: *The LORD God does nothing without revealing his plan to his servants the prophets.*

We too go on living, we have passed sixty-six. Perhaps because we live in an age when the average life span has considerably lengthened (in our countries). Perhaps because an operation delayed or removed the danger of death. Perhaps because of our genes or a robust constitution: *Seventy years is the span of our life, eighty if our strength holds* (Ps 90). The reasons are not important. Does this stage of our life have no other meaning? Is it just living to go on living? The Messiah has already come centuries ago, it is not for us to wait for him. Hope has been succeeded by memory, which is also a sign of our old age. On the other hand, if we refer to the second coming or parousia, this meeting will come in its own time. We must not hasten it or impatiently expect it. It is enough simply to watch out for it.

The objection or excuse does not hold. Let us look at it by examining the two comings. Jesus was born centuries ago. We have known old people who prolonged their lives to see an expected grandchild, their youngest daughter's first child, the first granddaughter after a number of grandsons. This is because the grandchild's birth is like a repetition of their own child's birth. In our spiritual life perhaps Christ is not yet fully born or needs to be born again. Or the Messiah who was born for us has not yet been born for people in our family, society, and it is up to us to be the midwives at this birth. An old person who has faith in Jesus Christ can spread it and communicate it, thereby multiplying Christ's birth. Like Anna the prophetess.

At the other extreme, we are awaiting our personal parousia, the final meeting with the glorified Christ. We can imagine that he comes or that we go or that both of us go out to meet each other . We have to prepare for this. We can fill the time that remains with preparations: we need to buy oil for the lamps, we have to sort out the business of the talents. And for this do we not have a counsellor and trusted friend in the Spirit of Christ, the Holy Spirit? He can explain many texts of the Bible with reference to ourselves. He can cultivate our sensitivity. Psalm 90:

[12]So make us know how few are our days
that our minds may learn wisdom.

He can kindle and enliven in us the love that makes us exclaim: *Come, Lord Jesus!* (Rev 22).

When at last the Messiah entered the temple, *Simeon took him in his arms and blessed the Lord*: the Old Testament supporting the New: sunset and dawn. Simeon weighed down and wrinkled, the child light and fresh. Who supports whom? This child who fills the old man's arms fills his whole life and his old age with meaning. Simeon's whole life is justified by this moment: it is the only one the Bible has recorded. At this moment Simeon's life is so full of meaning, that this page of the gospel does for a whole biography. In the same way as for this magnificent second temple the welcoming of this child is its highest privilege:

126

I shall fill this house with splendour, says the LORD of hosts... and the splendour of this latter house will surpass the splendour of the former (Hag 2:7).

Suddenly the Lord whom you seek will come to his temple; the messenger of the covenant in whom you delight is here (Mal 3:1).

If you who are meditating are a priest, think of the consecrated bread and wine which you raise before the congregation. Your tired arms holding the Messiah among his people, and with this gesture filling your last years with meaning. One day, suddenly our positions will change. We shall be children again in glory , and he will firmly carry us in his arms or take us by the hand to his Father and ours.

Simeon utters a blessing: *'Lord, now let your servant depart in peace, according to your word.'* To let a servant depart means releasing him, setting him free, in Old Testament legal language. Thus we find in the Exodus accounts and the Deuteronomy legislation.

Exodus:
5:1 Let my people go...
8:1 Let my people go...

Deuteronomy:
Should a fellow-Hebrew, be it a man or a woman, sell himself to you as a slave, he is to serve you for six years. In the seventh year you must set him free... Do not resent it when you have to set him free... (15:12-18)

See also the episode related in Jeremiah 34.
Simeon has been in the Lord's service since his youth

(in the temple?). He has been a faithful servant. Now the time for release has come: not freed from the Lord but freed from other duties. He sees death coming as a liberation or emancipation.

We read in the book of Job:

> 7:2Like those of a slave longing for the shade
> or a servant kept waiting for his wages.

The evening shade has come and pay for the day's work. Simeon has his wages in his arms. What a reward for the end of his life's day! The shade that will cover him and gently welcome him is the final shadow. Did Simeon hope for what we call eternal rest? It is not explicit in the text, but by then there were already many Jews who hoped for an after-life. When we make Simeon's words our own, we see death as liberation from the slavery of corruption. Romans:

> 8:20Humanity itself is to be freed from the shackles of mortality and is to enter upon the glorious liberty of the children of God.

According to your word. However sad we feel because we have to die, we are consoled by the promise of future immortality. *Lord, now let your servant depart in peace, according to your word.*

For my eyes have seen your salvation. Jesus said: *Blessed are the eyes that see what you see.* He also said: *Blessed are those who believe without seeing.* We have not physically seen the Saviour. Faith poured into us by the Spirit has shown him to us, contemplation has revealed him before our eyes. Our contemplative gaze has been with the mysteries of Christ's life, made us present and active, take part. Like an *unworthy servant* we have looked into the cave at Bethlehem. We have attended the death on the cross as if we were really present. Before the final vision beyond the grave, there are still mysteries for us to contemplate. The Old Testament said: *Nobody can see God and live*. John says: *No one has seen God*. Only in the other life beyond death will we be able to say in all truth: our eyes *have seen* and go on seeing *your salvation*.

You have set him before all nations. From this corner of the world, enclosed in the temple Simeon's gaze embraces the world. Isaiah:

> 40:5Then will the glory of the LORD be revealed
> and all mankind together will see it.
> 49:6It is too slight a task for you, as my servant,
> to restore the tribes of Jacob,
> to bring back the survivors of Israel.
> I shall appoint you a light to the nations
> so that my salvation may reach
> earth's farthest bounds.

This tiny child is a gigantic lighthouse reaching all horizons, a light to lighten the nations. We can apply the verse from Ecclesiasticus:

> 24:32I will again make learning shine like the dawn,
> that its light may be seen from afar.

It is a satellite that reaches all points of the globe. It is the *light of the world*. He is also the *glory of your people Israel*. The glory of Israel was the Lord. When they committed their crime on Sinai, the people *exchanged their Glory for the image of a bull that feeds on grass* (Ps 106). In Ezekiel the Glory departed from the temple where it resided; at the end of the book it returns. Simeon sees this Glory or divine presence in the child. Will the people of Israel accept him? Will the nations accept his light?

Simeon adds a dramatic reflection on human freedom, which can accept or refuse the light. The child will be a sign that will be rejected. Many in Israel will stand or fall because of him. Mary will be involved in the strife. What side have we been on? On the whole we have accepted the Messiah's light but we have shaded or dimmed its brightness in many ways.

Mary will be involved in her son's destiny. If we read Luke's phrase as a Semitic idiom (which is reasonable), Simeon's phrase means 'a sword on your neck' or 'knife at your throat.' (See Isaiah 53:12 for the literal version of the Hebrew 'he bared his neck'.) It is a prediction of physical or spiritual martyrdom. Marian spirituality has given Mary the title of martyr because of her intense sharing in her son's cross. According to the Semitic reading, Luke is the precursor of this idea, in Simeon's mouth.

There is something else: let us imagine the old man looking at the young mother so delighted with her son. He prophesies her son's glory, evoking all her love and tenderness. Now he prophesies struggle and martyrdom. Isn't he being cruel? The old man is the last Old Testament prophet and has to say what the Spirit inspires him to say.

Luke still has a little space left for old Phanuel's daughter Anna, from one of the least known tribes in the Bible. Let us say a word about this tribe, since Luke takes the trouble to mention it. Asher means Happy, because when their ancestor was born, his mother exclaimed: *'Happiness has come, for women will call me happy!'* Does this have anything to do with the scene described by Luke? Anna is not a talkative or gossipy old woman, because she spends her many words in prayers. What happens is that she cannot contain the news and *'talked about the child to all who were looking for the liberation of Jerusalem'*. The child is the Messiah, no less! What a pleasant way to pass from prayer to preaching, to be able to give the great news. Anna was not only a preacher but an 'evangelist', that is, bringer of good news. So there is still something left for old women to do or say.

Abraham
The first patriarch

Abraham is the great patriarch. He is not just an old man but a patriarch. It is not the same thing to be an old man and to be a patriarch. Being old is a matter of years, being a patriarch is a question of descent. Perhaps we may confuse the two and call a venerable old man a patriarch, especially if he has a fine white beard. Abraham is the first patriarch because, according to God's promise, a large nation descends from him. The patriarch is the common ancestor of a large tribe, Abraham is the common ancestor of many. Even though the Genesis text only gives him two sons, Ishmael and Isaac, nations *will be born from him.*

Are there patriarchs in our modern societies? Perhaps some families keep alive the memory of a common ancestor, from whom various branches sprang. This is exceptional, however, so we are going to return to the theme of age, which is what interests us here. It is true that in our modern societies old people are becoming more and more numerous. What the Bible thinks of as old age has become a common occurrence. If Psalm 90 tells us that the years of a human life are seventy and for the most robust, eighty, we have to admit that our species has become robust. As an example or as a theme for meditation, let us take a peep at the old man Abraham in a significant moment, which we read about in Genesis chapter 21.

Abraham had a son by his concubine Hagar, whom he called Ishmael. Legally he could have been considered as the heir. But the Lord had told Abraham that his heir would be a son by his wife, Sarah. Finally the son promised by God was born after a long wait by Abraham and Sarah. They called him Isaac which sounds like Smiling, Joyful or Festive. Sarah *danced for joy* and Abraham delighted in his renewed virility. We should not be surprised that the Bible tells us that the patriarch was a hundred years old when Isaac was born; in the matter of years the biblical narrator tends to be generous. He uses this round number to exalt the divine blessing of human fertility. The result is a suggestive figure: a biological father at an age to be a grandfather, at least. If a stranger came and congratulated the old man on being a grandfather, he would correct him with a touch of pride: father, you mean! And he would take the baby in his arms to feel its soft warm flesh against his cheeks, his flesh.

As was the custom in that culture, Sarah nursed her baby for two or three years. He has got over the illnesses and dangers of infancy and is weaned. The occasion is marked by a big party given by the patriarch. While the guests are at the banquet, little Isaac begins playing with his elder brother, Ishmael. The biblical narrator fastens on this moment: two brothers playing, Abraham looks on, Sarah considers. What does Abraham feel? What does an old man feel when he sees children playing? What does he feel if they are his grandchildren? It is a very different thing to watch children playing sponta- neously and games regimented by professionals. The old man watches the children at play without inhibitions. He appreciates the grace of their movements, their agile imaginative leaps, and he smiles. After a while he joins in. Mentally the old man returns to his childhood with a bitter sweet pleasure. He feels nostalgic for a time long past and enjoys his life which still continues. And if they are not his children or grandchildren? There is always a human bond between an old person and a child.

Sarah's reaction is different: Isaac is her son, Ishmael the concubine's. If the children play together they will become close as brothers. One day the slave woman's son will claim part of the inheritance equal to that of his brother. Who knows if he will claim rights due to him for being the first-born and having been legally recognised. Sarah is jealous of Ishmael, she is not able to enjoy watching them play. Her self-interest strangles her pleasure, calculation rules and she demands that her husband should expel the concubine and her son. 'This greatly *distressed Abraham because the slave girl's child was his son too.*' Both Isaac and Ishmael can continue his line.

This is a moment for meditation both for old men and old women, because it is not a question of sex but of age and attitude. Do children playing irritate us? They are noisy, they do not respect granny or grandpa, they disturb our rest, they are a nuisance. I think children's games are a test for an old person. Perhaps you do not feel like joining in physical games. But you can join in games of imagination. Imagination is the basis of play. Imagination can be a sign of spiritual vitality, a sign of childhood regained. The child is serious and trusting when he asks the old person to play with him, that is, enter into his fantasy world. The old person will go along with the fantasy in full awareness, watching what he does. When he was a child he entered totally into the spirit of the game and was unaware of his creativity. The old can make this final discovery: something from their past life, which they had not consciously reflected on, is now being projected in the child for their contemplation.

If that is not sufficient, let us take another bold step, with the help of another biblical text. The book of

Proverbs show Wisdom (*sophia* in Greek, *hokma* in Hebrew) personified in the figure of a little girl who joins in the work of God her father as an apprentice. After she has delighted him with her games she suggests she goes down to the sphere of earth and play with humans. Proverbs:

8:30Then I was at his side each day,
his darling and delight,
playing in his presence continually,
playing over his whole world,
while my delight was mankind.

Christian tradition has identified this poetic personification with the person of Jesus Christ who collaborates with the Father in creation and one day descends to the realm of humanity to play with them: the natural Son with the adoptive children.

Even though the gospels do not mention it, it is legitimate and can be fruitful to imagine the child Jesus playing at home or with his friends. Paul insists that he was made like us in everything except sin. One human quality is our ability to play. Humanity has been called *homo ludens*. Jesus' childhood experience may have been the source of the comparison quoted by Luke:

7:32They are like children sitting in the market-place
and calling to each other:
We played the pipes for you
and you wouldn't dance.
We sang sad songs,
and you wouldn't cry.

The reproach is for not joining in the game. Had Jesus heard one of his friends say: I'm not going to play? He recommends that we should become like children. Well, what better way is there to become like children than by playing?

And what will happen if one day the adoptive children want to inherit too? Fine. There is no Sarah to go against it: they will be heirs of God and co-heirs with Christ.

Isaac
Father of two nations

According to the Bible family tree, Isaac is the second patriarch in the central trunk. According to tradition his brother Ishmael is the ancestor of the Arabs. Isaac has only one wife (hence he is preferred as a symbol or type of Christ). For many years his wife gives him no children and the promised succession is threatened. So, when he was forty he prayed for his wife and obtained the gift of fertility for her. She bore not one child, but twins. The narrator jokingly refers to Esau's ugliness when he was born, because he thinks of him as the ancestor of the Edomites. Jacob is born grasping Esau's heel. These details foretell the character and destiny of the two infants. The boys grow and when they are of age they choose jobs: Esau became a hunter, Jacob a shepherd. After this summary of what is to come, let us concentrate on the father.

In the family quadrilateral (we could call it a modern family with only two children) an alignment of forces develops based on preferences. The father prefers the elder (elder by minutes or hours), the mother prefers the younger. It is not strange that the mother prefers the younger, the more homebound. Neither is it strange that the father prefers the first-born, even by such a short time. What is strange is the reason given by the narrator: *Isaac preferred Esau, for he had a taste for wild game* (25:28). A not very sensible gastronomic preference! To prefer a game stew to a dish of lamb is reasonable, but to prefer a son for this reason appears excessive. The fact will turn against Isaac when he is old. This is the moment we are going to catch him, as we read an extraordinary account, which I shall not comment upon extensively here.

It is the story of the blessing which will establish the legitimate heir. With his mother's complicity, the younger son tricks his old father and gets the blessing which belongs to the elder. The mother exploits her husband's almost childish weakness for game stew. Lured by the fake stew, deceived by the hairy feel of Jacob, ravished by the aroma of wild herbs, the blind old man gives his blessing to Jacob, mistaking him for Esau. Why did he not trust his hearing now that his sight was failing? Why did not the sound of the voice mean as much as his fumbling touch? The old man is conditioned by his previous behaviour and does not rise above himself at this crucial moment. He is senile, infantile.

Thus he divides the inheritance between the two. The younger son gets the legitimate line, fertile fields (although he was a shepherd), political dominance over his brother. The elder gets open country, the sword and a fight for independence, which one day he will win. The sword is not a hunting weapon but for war. Is he justified in his fight for independence? I don't know whether Isaac is hinting at vengeance, when he announces to Esau that one day he will shake off the yoke. At the moment I want to concentrate on the narrative without going into the author's further intentions, although these are important in another context.

This is the heritage left by Isaac: sanction for deceit as a fait accompli, two brothers divided by hatred and desire for vengeance, a political future of domination and violence. In contrast, his presence in life delays the tragedies. When after a good number of years he dies, the reconciled brothers will perform his funeral rites.

In our day the problem of succession and inheritance is not usually so crucial as in the Genesis stories. Matters are settled by legal channels which are fairly conventional – financial matters, that is to say, which are not the only or most important concerns. Today too there are dramatic legacies where there are enormous fortunes. But these are exceptional cases we read about in the newspapers. This is not what ordinarily occurs. So does the portrait of Isaac have nothing to tell us? Inheritance includes other things besides financial. They are no less important. What spiritual legacy will we leave? A united or divided family? Will we pass on our senile and capricious preferences to our descendants? Even though we are retired, our physical and spiritual presence can count in the family and a wider circle. Let us think about what we shall leave behind us when we have finally and irrevocably retired. Let it not be: 'after me the deluge.' Or the selfish remark of King Hezekiah when he is told of the future sacking of Jerusalem. He shrugs his shoulders saying: *'There will be peace and security in my lifetime'* (Is 39:8).

A biblical man, partly through ignorance of a future life, left another precious legacy, his good name, his fame after death — Ecclesiasticus:

> 37:26 A person who is wise will possess the confidence of his people and his name will live for ever.
> 39:11 If he lives long, he will leave a name in a thousand; when he goes to his long rest, his reputation is secure.
> 41:11 Take thought for your name: it will outlive you longer than thousands of great hoards of gold.
> 13 The days of a good life are numbered,
> but a good name lasts for all time.

Even though we hope for another life, wouldn't we like to leave a good memory behind us? Proverbs expresses it thus: *Blessed is the memory of the honest*. We have the expression 'of happy memory.'

We may imagine that if Isaac was old, Rebecca was a little less old. We gather from the biblical account that she still ran the household. How does she do this? By plotting and advancing her preferences against established custom. She does not just collude in deceiving her husband but cynically assumes responsibility for it. The consequences of her action are that, in order not to lose both her sons in one day, she has to give up the presence of her youngest and she does not know when she will see him again. Nevertheless, Rebecca is a matriarch in Israel and her matriarchy extends to another neighbouring and rival people.

Leaping forward over generations, one day we see Jesus the Jew and Herod the Edomite standing face to face: Jacob and Esau again. Now the positions have changed and an Edomite king reigns over the Jews. A Herod intent on eliminating the expected rival king. Another Herod will sit in judgment, mocking and despising this man who looks so little like a king. But the new Jacob does not cheat, he does not usurp kingdoms, rob legacies or blessings. Jesus, the new Jacob, is his Father's beloved Son, the legitimate heir. He comes to share his prodigious inheritance with his new brothers. By making us his brothers and sisters he makes his Father the greatest patriarch of all, 'from whom all fatherhood on earth takes its name.'

Jacob
Mediator of divine blessings

In the biblical scheme Jacob is the third member of the great patriarchal trunk. From him the trunk branches outwards into twelve branches or brothers, or tribes. Let us pass over his story as a boy and young man, because we want to see him in old age (which began much earlier for Israelites). I shall assume that you are familiar with the text and have it to hand and therefore proceed partly by allusions and summaries.

Jacob either did not learn from or has forgotten his family experience and so the fatal preferences recur. Among the twelve brothers he prefers Joseph *because he was a child of his old age*. Jacob had had twelve children from his two wives and two concubines. Joseph was the first by his favourite wife, Rachel, and Benjamin was the second. His fatherly tenderness gathers force like a slow wave and falls tumultuously on Joseph. He shows his preference ostentatiously. Joseph has a better coat than his brothers and spends more time at home. The father's preference and Joseph's famous dreams provoke the envy and hatred of his brothers. Is Jacob unaware of the explosive situation? When he hears Joseph telling his dreams he lends a fatherly ear and ponders what they could mean. Are they oracles about the future? Are they simply projected wishes? Ecclesiasticus:

> 34:1 Vain hopes delude the senseless,
> and dreams give wings to a fool's fancy.
> 2 Paying heed to dreams
> is like clutching a shadow or chasing the wind.

³What you see in a dream is nothing but a
    reflection,
the image of a face in a mirror.
⁴Truth can no more come from illusion
than purity can come from impurity.
⁵Divination, omens, and dreams are all futile,
mere fantasies, like those of a woman in labour.
⁶Unless they are sent by intervention from the Most
    High,
pay no attention to them.
⁷Dreams have led many astray
and disappointed those who built their hopes on
    them.

Jacob wants to understand this secret world glimpsed by his son, but he does not seem to want to understand the everyday world in his family.

Tension grows until it explodes in violence. Joseph's brothers contemplate murder. When Joseph is taken for a slave do his dreams stop or do they begin to be fulfilled?

Let us return to Jacob, an old man by biblical standards. The poor man is enmeshed in a web of ignorance and false suppositions. He thinks his favourite son is dead, torn to pieces by a wild beast. There is the evidence of his special coat drenched with blood. This is both false and true because the wild beast of hatred has attacked the defenceless boy, who had provoked his brothers' violence. Although he is certain that his son is dead, and even though beforehand he had reflected on Joseph's dreams, now Jacob does not stop to think about the reason for what has occurred because he does not really know what is going on in his family. Jacob accepts Joseph's death as an irreparable fact and no longer looks forward to the future. He surrenders to morbid grieving as if asking it to bring him death. His ignorance of his family covers all his children, except perhaps Benjamin. They come to console him in a macabre mourning ceremony. Jacob is incapable of seeing through the farce and thereby stores up new grief for himself. In reality the family is broken, the tree and patriarchal branches are damaged by the storm. Jacob lives on in his fog of ignorance and false suppositions. He devotes himself to licking his wounds and almost revelling in them.

Nevertheless his paternal presence still goes on giving welcome shade or communicating active sap, which leads his sons towards reconciliation. Throughout the chain of meetings in Egypt their father is present and active. He still resists letting Benjamin go because he is afraid of losing him. Finally he gives in to his sons' arguments. He is also becoming more reasonable, even though he does not emerge from his ignorance. As a father Jacob is the catalyst for the transformation of his children. But through his blindness he cannot consciously assist in the process.

I have commented on this story elsewhere focussing on brotherhood. Here I shall concentrate on the old man. Far away Joseph grows up and gets on, he marries and has children, he becomes vizier of Egypt, he saves the country and feeds other nations. Joseph is grown up and his father is an old man. We are invited to be present at their meeting:

When they told him that Joseph was still alive and was ruler of the whole of Egypt, he was stunned at the news and did not believe them. However when they reported to him all that Joseph had said to them, and when he saw the wagons which Joseph had provided to fetch him, his spirit revived. Israel said, 'It is enough! Joseph my son is still alive; I shall go and see him before I die' (Gen 45:26).

In his mind he has a picture of Joseph as a bright and not very powerful adolescent. Added to this he has another fantasy of Joseph torn to pieces by a wild beast. It is possible, perhaps, even easy to delete the blood stains and recover the original picture. Will the present Joseph correspond to this picture? The present Joseph is a man who gives Jacob grandchildren and a powerful politician who gives him his protection. He has at his command wagons, servants and can give orders. But above or beneath all this, he is Jacob's flesh-and-blood Joseph he can hold in his arms:

> They entered Goshen, and Joseph had his chariot yoked to go up there to meet Israel his father. When they met, Joseph threw his arms round him and wept on his shoulder for a long time. Israel said to Joseph, 'I have seen for myself that you are still alive. Now I am ready to die' (Gen 46:29).

At such a moment basic values are recovered or revealed. Neither power nor triumph matter, only that his son is alive. The tears dissolve many years' sorrows, a single minute's embrace makes up for years of separation. He thought he was dead; it is as if he had risen from the dead.

While they are embracing let us pause for reflection. After years of absence in this mortal life, what will it be like to embrace Christ our brother, a human being like us, risen from the dead, alive and in glory? True, there is a difference. We did not think he was dead, we believe in his resurrection and hope to share in it. But there is another difference greater than this and that is the incomparable value of this eldest child of our humanity, his unutterable glory. We go to meet him and he comes to meet us. Times passes, the distance grows shorter. Until it vanishes in a final embrace.

Our old man has another meeting: his personal visit to Pharaoh. He is a mighty king, the heir of a tradition almost a thousand years old, whereas Jacob is a foreign bedouin, an emigrant. Joseph, the vizier, performs the introduction:

Then Joseph brought his father in and presented him to Pharaoh. Jacob blessed Pharaoh, who asked him his age, and he answered, 'The years of my life on earth are one hundred and thirty; few and hard have they been — fewer than the years my fathers lived.' Jacob then blessed Pharaoh and withdrew from his presence (Gen 47:7-9).

What interests us is the ancient patriarch's blessing. His long life (we need not take too much notice of the exact figures) is an effect and sign of divine blessing. His advanced age confers on him an almost priestly dignity, as a mediator of divine blessings. Pharaoh, his superior in rank and power, recognises his superiority in years and accepts the stranger's blessing. To the blessing of his years is added his particular patriarchal blessing, which Joseph is heir to: *All the nations of the earth will bless themselves by you and your descendants* (Gen 28:14). As well as this there is the blessing Jacob wrested in his fight with the divine being (Gen 32).

Happy is the old person who throughout his life or in moments of struggle with his God has accumulated blessings he can pass on. An old person like this is a channel of blessings in a family or community. There are children who do not understand, perhaps giving economic or sociological reasons as their pretext. Thus they deprive themselves of blessings in their family life and at work. Of course an old person should not boast of his years, even though he modestly confesses: *they have been few and hard*. After all what are eighty or ninety years? *Few and hard*. Psalm 90 says: *at their best they are but toil and sorrow, for they pass quickly and we vanish*. In spite of everything Jacob is the bearer of divine blessings and every old person can be so who is capable of receiving and administering them.

We are left with the final act, which is not related in the Bible text when it happens but is alluded to later. We read the text in Genesis 50:15-17:

Now that their father was dead, Joseph's brothers were afraid, for they said, 'What if Joseph should bear a grudge against us and pay us back for all the harm we did to him?' They therefore sent a messenger to Joseph to say, 'In his last words to us before he died, your father gave us this message: 'Say this to Joseph: I ask you to forgive your brothers' crime and wickedness; I know they did you harm.' So now we beg you: forgive our crime, for we are servants of your father's God.'

From this we deduce that Jacob had been told about everything that had happened. What is done cannot be undone; but before he dies Jacob wants to assure the legacy of a family of united brothers. He too was at one time violently separated from his twin brother, largely through his own fault. But he had managed to become reconciled with Esau and when Isaac their father died, the two brothers were together at his burial. Perhaps this memory affects him, perhaps by now this experience has been assimilated as part of what he has become. They were twin brothers and found it difficult to agree. Now there are twelve children from four mothers. Together they are to carry forward the history of a family which will be a nation one day. Unity is essential. Therefore Jacob's last message is forgiveness and reconciliation. Joseph accepted and carried out his father's last wish and hence what had been woven with evil turned to good, resulting in life for a *numerous people*.

On his death bed the father asked his son to forgive his guilty brothers. On his death bed on the cross the Son asked his Father to forgive: *for they do not know what they do.*' And the brother's violent death becomes a source of life for a numerous people.

Anyone, young or old, who lives because he has been forgiven, must also know how to forgive: only thus can he die in peace. Forgive us our trespasses as we forgive those who trespass against us.

Moses
Man with a mission

I have written a book about Moses' mission, including his retirement and death.* So I do not want to repeat a lot of this here. Nevertheless I think that some of it can be summarised and there is still something to say about his old age. Above all we should not make things difficult for ourselves with the biblical numbers. Deuteronomy 34:7 says that Moses died when he was a hundred and twenty years old, at the end of the wanderings through the desert, which lasted forty years. This means he must have set out on this adventure when he was eighty. Does this mean he was an old man when he left Horeb to present himself to Pharaoh? When he left Pharaoh's court we imagine he was young, robust and of marriage-able age. Let us put him at a bit over twenty. Does this mean he lived for sixty years in Midian? Highly unlikely. It is better to leave the narrator to his numbers and for us to observe the character in his old age.

Moses is a man with a mission for which he has God's trust. His mission is to bring the people out from slavery in Egypt, to unite them in a covenant with the Lord and lead them and settle them in the promised land. The mission encounters numerous obstacles, which Moses overcomes with vigour and tenacity and help from God. Unexpectedly the intermediate stage in the desert which could have taken a few months is prolonged for forty years, during which we may imagine that Moses the

*Moses: his mission, trans. D. Livingstone, St Paul Publications, Slough, UK 1990.

148

mature man ages, even though Deuteronomy 37:7 tells us that *his sight was undimmed and his vigour unimpaired.*

Difficulties in leading the people physically and spiritually were only to be expected. Although Moses sometimes feels discouraged, the Lord comforts him with his help. The terrible, unexpected thing is what happens at the end when the people are about to settle in the territory of Canaan. Moses has led the people to the frontier, to the opposite bank of the Jordan. He is strong and vigorous and has no diseases. His prestige and leadership are intact and increased. All that is left to do is to go in. But Moses' death is hastened and he, in whom the Lord confides, receives the warning to prepare to die.

In Moses as an old and dying man we learn that a mission can take longer than the lifetime of even a long-lived person. It is not enough to set up an enterprise and lead it but it is also necessary to foster successors who can continue and conclude it. Can the old man say: I have fulfilled my mission? Or shouldn't he say: I have finished the part assigned to me of a mission that is greater than me. Moses is able to do this by fulfilling the Lord's orders. On one occasion in Numbers 11, God takes part of his spirit or charisma and shares it among seventy collaborators for collegiate government. On another occasion when God tells him he is going to die, Moses is worried about the work continuing. We need to read the text slowly in order to appreciate Moses' greatness as an old man:

The Lord said to Moses, 'Go up this mountain, Mount Abarim, and view the land which I have given to the Israelites. Then, when you have seen it, you too will be gathered to your father's kin as was your brother Aaron; for you and Aaron disobeyed my command when the community disputed with me in the wilderness of Zin:

you did not uphold my holiness before them at the waters.' (They were the waters of Meribah-ny-Kadesh in the wilderness of Zin.)

Then Moses said to the LORD, 'Let the LORD, the God of the spirits of all mankind appoint a man over the community to go out and come in at their head, to lead them out and bring them home, so that the community of the LORD may not be like sheep without a shepherd.' The LORD answered, 'Take Joshua son of Nun, a man powerful in spirit; lay your hand on him and have him stand before Eleazar the priest and all in their presence, and delegate some of your authority to him, so that the entire Israelite community will obey him. He must present himself before Eleazar the priest, who will obtain a decision for him by consulting the Urim before the LORD; at his word they are to go out and come home, both Joshua and the whole community of the Israelites.

Moses did as the LORD had commanded him. He took Joshua, presented him to Eleazar the priest and the whole community, laid his hands on him, and gave him his commission, as instructed by the LORD (Num 27:12-23).

Moses delegates part of his authority to him, associates him with his task. He does not put him in reserve having only the right of succession. He is not jealous of Joshua or of his own authority. On a day soon to come the Lord will tell Joshua: *Today I will begin to make you greater in front of all Israel, so that they see I am with you as I was with Moses.*

There are old people who are not capable of associating with a successor in their work or mission. They are jealous of their authority, they keep a monopoly of decisions. They begin by identifying with a task; they end up identifying the task with themselves. Like those archaic and exotic monarchs who buried their wives and servants with them. Samson died killing his enemies; these people die killing all their competitors or successors. They do not understand they had a role in the world and this function continues.

Sometimes we think of history as a mere succession of generations. The biblical expression 'from generation to generation' or 'generation after generation' seems to invite this. In fact the succession of generations is not like this, they overlap. One generation is not over, merely reaching maturity, when a second generation begins and the two live together; they share a time span together. And as they grow on yet another generation is born... There is contemporaneity in the succession of generations. Hence the principle of associating one's successor in one's work, making him a contemporary. Whereas to those who will succeed us when we are well and truly dead we can bequeath other things: writings, works, memories. We do not associate them with our affairs. In other words, an old person does not possess a monopoly of a period of years. He shares them with others.

Moses does not retire but death retires him at a stroke. We have known people whose retirement brought or hastened their death: they were unable or did not want to live without a job to do. Moses is the opposite; death is his retirement. The biblical narrator wants to give this death dramatic grandeur. I doubt there is anything like it in the whole of the Old Testament. Read the end of Deuteronomy, the last book of the Pentateuch, which Jews call the Torah:

Moses went up from the lowlands of Moab to Mount Nebo, to the top of Pisgah eastwards from Jericho, and the LORD showed him the whole land, from Gilead to Dan; the whole of Naphtali; the territory of Ephraim and Manasseh, the Negeb and the plain; the valley of Jericho, city of palm trees, as far as Zoar. The LORD said to him,

'This is the land which I swore to Abraham, Isaac and Jacob that I would give to their descendants. I have let you see it with your own eyes, but you will not cross over into it.' There in the Moabite country, Moses the servant of the LORD died, as the LORD had said (Deut 34:1-5).

Moses' time has come. Time in the Hebrew expression: to be 'gathered to his own', that is, go down into the grave or dwelling place of the dead. Before this final descent Moses is invited to go up the highest mountain in the area, Mount Nebo. This is his second mountain; his first was Sinai, where he met the LORD for the first time and returned to meet him again to receive the rules of the covenant. His ascent now is for another reason: to contemplate. From the peak, facing west, Moses gazes at the future, not his own, but that of his people. The promised land is Israel's near and remote future. Moses closes his eyes which are filled with the future, with hope. As if when he is 'gathered to his own', his ancestors, it will be to tell them what he has seen. (However this is not a Hebrew way of thinking, but our own reflection.) Moses' final yearning is not for an irrecoverable past but for an expected future.

For us the situation is different. For us 'being gathered to our own' means going up to our Father's house, higher than any mountain and with a limitless panorama. It is our final meeting: not to go down but up. But we still gaze for a last time at our family we leave behind: let it be a hopeful gaze. There are parts or periods of history which we will not live through in this world. May they have something of the promised land for those we leave as we depart for new spaces. If our old age is a spiritual ascent, in spite of physical decay, we can see or glimpse a future, which is not for us, but in a way it does belong to us because we helped prepare it, because we led others to it.

From the height of the cross before he died, what view did Jesus contemplate? How does it broaden for him when he ascends into heaven?

I am no longer in the world; they are still in the world, but I am coming to you, Holy Father, protect them by the power of your name, the name you have given me, that they may be one, as we are one... Now I am coming to you; but while I am still in the world I speak these words so that they may have my joy within them in full measure... It is not for these alone that I pray but for those also who through their words put their faith in me... Father, they are your gift to me; and my desire is that they may be with me where I am, so that they may look upon my glory, which you have given me because you loved me before the world began (Jn 17:11-24).

Barzillai
Sensible to the end

The old man Barzillai acts twice during Absalom's rebellion. The first time is when David flees to him, abandoning the initiative to his rebellious son. Barzillai with others shows his loyalty to the king, thereby risking his future. We read about it in 2 Samuel 17:28:

> They brought mattresses and blankets, bowls and jugs. They brought also wheat and barley, flour and roasted grain, beans and lentils, honey and curds, sheep and fat cattle, and offered them to David and his people to eat, knowing that the people must be hungry and thirsty and weary in the wilderness.

The second time is after Absalom's defeat. David is about to cross the Jordan to go back to Jerusalem: *I know now that I am king of Israel* (19:22) Together with the priest Zadok and Abiathar, General Amasa, Shimei and Meribaal, we find the old man Barzillai:

> Barzillai the Gileadite too had come down from Rogelim, and he went as far as the Jordan with the king to escort him on his way. Barzillai was very old, eighty years of age; it was he who had provided for the king while he was at Mahanaim, for he was a man of great wealth. The king said to Barzillai, 'Cross over with me and I shall provide for you in my household in Jerusalem.' Barzillai answered, 'Your servant is far too old to go up with Your Majesty to

Jerusalem. I am now eighty years old. I cannot tell what is pleasant and what is not; I cannot taste what I eat or drink; I can no longer listen to the voices of men and women singing. Why should I be a further burden on Your Majesty? Your servant will attend the king for a short way across the Jordan; and why should the king reward me so handsomely? Let me go back and end my days in my own town near the grave of my father and mother. Here is my son Kimham; let him cross over with Your Majesty and do for him what you think best.' The king answered, 'Let Kimham cross with me, and I shall do for him whatever you think best; and I shall do for you whatever you ask' (2 Sam 19:32-38).

Barzillai prefers the quietness of his own town to the bustle of the court. He is well off and does not need a royal pension. As for the pleasures of the court, good food and good music, he can no longer appreciate or enjoy them. Barzillai judges clearly and sensibly. Old people are tempted to run down things they no longer enjoy: 'things were better in my time, it's not like it was, how dreary...' Barzillai is not making culinary or artistic judgments. He acknowledges the lack is in himself. He accepts the situation serenely and is content to have a bit of peace before he dies.

Barzillai appears a couple of times in sacred history to give us an unintentional lesson in good sense. His words takes us by the hand to another illustrious old man, who merits a chapter to himself: Qohelet or Ecclesiastes.

Ecclesiastes
The lightness of being

We usually use an article with his name because the Hebrew word sounds like a title: The Preacher or The President of the Assembly. Ecclesiastes is a Greek word which attempts to translate the Hebrew term *Qohelet*. We do not know his real name or age. Presenting himself as a king and David's son is a literary fiction. We deduce from his pages that he was very probably an old man.

His project is to weigh up human life: its meaning and value. In order not to speak from hearsay he makes systematic tests, or pretends to do so attributing them to the fictitious Solomon. What he lacks in personal experience he makes up for by a lot of observation and reflection. We sometimes say: 'It's no good dwelling on it.' Ecclesiastes' theme seems to be: 'We should dwell on it.' His favourite verb seems to be *ra'iti*, meaning I have seen, I have observed, sometimes I have experienced. He also uses the verb *sabti*, which means I have turned back to, I have repeated; sometimes it is *sabboti*, meaning, I have turned over, revolved (the matter). He distils a whole account of human life in eighteen pages of the Hebrew Bible. Isn't this over-ambitious? Because he goes on distilling until he gets to the quintessence, a phrase he repeats as a refrain: 'utter futility, everything is futile.' Developing the phrase a little but condensing the whole work, here I shall offer something in between: life is a perpetual and monotonous going round and round, life is a pendulum that swings between opposites. Human beings invent forgetfulness in order to take for new what is already experienced or known. The swing of the pendulum makes both extremes relative.

Let us begin by reading two sections, almost prose poems, which are characteristic of the author's style. (I have quoted part of the second passage in my commentary on Psalm 30). The first passage is from chapter 1:

[4]Generations come and generations go,
while the earth endures for ever.
[5]The sun rises and the sun goes down;
then it speeds to its place and rises there again.
[6]The wind blows to the south, it veers to the north;
round and round it goes and returns full circle.
[7]All streams run to the sea;
yet the sea never overflows.
Back to the place from which the streams ran
they return to run again.
[8]All things are wearisome.
No one can describe them all,
no eye can see them all,
no ear can hear them all.
[9]What has happened will happen again,
what has been done will be done again;
there is nothing new under the sun.

The second passage comes at the beginning of chapter 3:

[1]For everything its season;
and for every activity under the sun its time:
[2]a time to be born, a time to die;
a time to plant and a time to uproot;
[3]a time to kill and a time to heal;
a time to break down and a time to build up;
[4]a time to weep and a time to laugh;
a time for mourning and a time for dancing;

[5]a time to scatter stones and a time to gather them;
a time to embrace and a time to abstain from
  embracing;
[6]a time to seek and a time to lose;
a time to keep and a time to discard;
[7]a time to tear and a time to mend;
a time for silence and a time for speech;
[8]a time to love and a time to hate;
a time for war and a time for peace.

Before we go further into the book, here are two warnings. It is not for young people. Let us set the lower age limit at forty. Even though we may have read it or even studied it before, let us now try reading it slowly in our old age. The second warning is more important because it gives a key to the reading. The author's spiritual horizon and ours are substantially different. As we are not intending to retreat from our viewpoint, our reading will be critical. Thus we may reach a certain agreement ... for very different reasons.

The author thinks: death makes everyone equal, nothing that ends is worth very much. Death is the end and there is nothing after it. Therefore life is utter futility. We say: life is limited, this life ends in death, after that comes another incomparably better life. Therefore this life is futile: brief as a puff of air, light as a feather. In his novel *The Unbearable Lightness of Being*, Milan Kundera begins with a brief essay: Life is a continual novelty of unforeseeable events, which are not repeated and therefore have no consistency. It is because of this lack of consistency, this lightness, that existence is such heavy going. (Lightness could be another translation of the Hebrew *hebel*). The biblical author's evaluation is different; in fact the opposite: the lightness of human existence comes from its monotonous repetition and its

ending in death. In our Christian view the lightness/
futility of human life is comparative — in comparison
with the other life we hope for. Neither *Qohelet* nor
Kundera expect anything beyond death.

In his Letter to the Romans (8:18) Paul says that *the
sufferings we now endure bear no comparison with the
glory, as yet unrevealed, which is in store for us.* In 2
Corinthians 4:17 he says: *Our troubles are slight and
short-lived, and their outcome is an eternal glory which
far outweighs them.* Paul puts present sufferings and
future glory in the balance. The former are light and
ephemeral, the latter overwhelming. Let us make another
complementary test: if we put all the pleasures and
delights of this life on the scales, they would also weigh
little against the blessedness to come. These are our
terms of reference for a critical and enjoyable reading of
Ecclesiastes.

There is nothing new under the sun. It is true, compared with the newness of Christ everything is old or a
repeat. And when he *renews heaven and earth* the
newness will embrace the sun and will not be under it. *So
I applied my mind to understanding wisdom and
knowledge, madness and folly, and I came to see that this
too is a chasing of the wind* (1:17). It is true: compared to
God's wisdom revealed in Christ, compared with our
future knowledge of God, plainly, face to face.

*I considered my handiwork, all my labour and toil: it
was futility, all of it, and a chasing of the wind* (2:11). I
came to hate all my labour and toil here under the sun,
since I should have to leave it to my successor (2:18).
That is true, but there are works that accompany those
who die faithful to the Lord (Rev 14:13). There are
works that we call meritorious through the power of the
Spirit.

The author also bewails the injustices others suffer:

Where justice ought to be there was wickedness (3:16). *I saw the tears of the oppressed, and there was no one to comfort them* (4:1). This is the value of life in this world; but is it enough just to lament it? Can we not do something to remedy it? At our age perhaps all we can do is make others aware of it. Make those who are young and active aware of the situation and the challenge it offers. If we suppress the horizon of the other life, Ecclesiastes is right in his desolate weighing-up.

Everything that confronts them, everything is futile, since one and the same fate comes to all, just and unjust alike, good and bad, ritually clean and unclean, to the one who offers sacrifice and to the one who does not. The good and the sinner fare alike, he who can take an oath and he who dares not. This is what is wrong in all that is done here under the sun (9:2-3).

We could go on like this through pages of this book while we weigh up our own life. So what taste does it leave in our mouth, how does it weigh in our hands, what echo does it leave in our mind? In our own life has there been a balance between joy and suffering, success and failure, dream and reality? If we do not look forwards and upwards, perhaps we remain disenchanted, disappointed: utter futility, utter lightness. But when we have reached this balancing point, let us make a jump. Precisely this disenchantment and dissatisfaction make us look up higher. Then Ecclesiastes with all his emotional ashes will urge us on to seek for something that transcends this life under the sun.

Before we leave this disturbing thinker, let us read the last page of his book in two sections. Part 1 is advice to the young. Youth is ephemeral, do not despise but enjoy it, with responsibility towards God. Chapter 11:

7The light of day is sweet,
and pleasant to the eye is the sight of the sun.
8However many years a person may live
he should rejoice in all of them.
But let him remember the days of darkness,
for they will be many.
Everything that is to come will be futility.

9Delight in your youth, young man,
make the most of your early days;
let your heart and your eyes show you the way;
but remember that for all these things
God will call you to account.
10Banish vexation from your mind,
and shake off the troubles of the body,
for youth and the prime of life are mere futility.

The first verse extends to the whole of life the advice then given particularly for youth. Because there is a proportion: what youth is to the rest of life, this and much less is the rest of life compared with the 'days of darkness.' Hence the advice to enjoy, which in the context of this book means a moderate enjoyment without excesses.

The second text is the famous allegorical description of old age as a house falling to bits. Beside the text I will give the probable explanation of the images. The reader can consult this or make his own interpretation. Chapter 12:

1Remember your Creator in the days of your youth,
before the bad times come,
and the years draw near when you will say,
'I have no pleasure in them';
2before the sun and the light of day

give place to darkness,
before the moon and the stars grow dim,
and the clouds return with the rain.
[3]Remember him in the day
when the guardians of the house become unsteady
    (arms?),
and the strong men stoop (legs?),
when the women grinding the meal
cease work because they are few (teeth?),
and those who look through the windows
can see no longer (eyes),
[4]when the street doors are shut;
when the sound of the mill fades (ears),
when the chirping of the sparrow grows faint,
and the song-birds fall silent;
[5]when people are afraid of a steep place,
and the street is full of terrors;
when the blossom whitens on the almond tree
    (white hair?)
and the locust can only crawl (sex?)
and the caper buds no longer give zest.
For mortals depart to their everlasting home,
and the mourners go about the street.
[6]Remember your Creator
before the silver cord is snapped,
and the golden bowl is broken;
before the pitcher is shattered at the spring,
and the wheel broken at the well,
[7]before the dust returns to the earth as it began,
and the spirit returns to God who gave it.
[8]Utter futility, says the Preacher,
everything is futile.

Hezekiah
God knows best

Today we are going to introduce the story of a young man barely twenty years old. Isn't this out of place in a series of old people? When Hezekiah fell seriously ill he was a young man. When he died he was thirty five. So why are we giving him a place in these pages? Because his illness can serve as an example to us.

2 Kings 20 and Isaiah 38 tell us that Hezekiah fell mortally ill. The narrator knows this but the young king probably does not. Someone has to explain the situation clearly to him. Because a king has obligations to the state. It falls to the prophet Isaiah to inform the king on God's behalf. Isaiah 38:

[1]Give your last instructions to your household, for you are dying; you will not recover.

This is not just a medical diagnosis. It is not simply that a man of standing has to give the news to the king. Isaiah is God's instrument. His words are not diagnostic but an oracle. From the first verse onwards the reader is involved in the process in a religious way. Isaiah does not denounce the king's sins, he does not proclaim that he is dying as a punishment. It is a natural event, although it has been foreseen by God.

The young king reacts in the same context. There are psalms for the sick in which the psalmist accepts his sickness as the punishment of a certain sin and asks God to forgive him and cure him. Hezekiah does not have sins to confess as possible causes for his illness. He does not take the illness as a punishment, but as a fatality. But he knows that someone controls this physical fatality. So:

> Hezekiah turned his face to the wall and offered this prayer to the Lord: 'LORD, remember how I have lived before you, faithful and loyal in your service, always doing what was pleasing to you.' And he wept bitterly (Is 38: 2-3).

The Lord hears him and sends him an answer through the prophet, thus keeping the whole process in his hands. The narrator makes us feel this at every stage, so that we do not leave the religious sphere.

> Then the word of the LORD came to Isaiah: 'Go and say to Hezekiah: "This is the word of the LORD the God of your father David: I have heard your prayer and seen your tears;"' I am going to add fifteen years to your life (Is 38:4).

He simply announces *I am going to add*. God keeps control, without resorting to a miracle. It is not like Naman bathing seven times in the Jordan to cure himself of a skin disease. Isaiah does not receive instructions from God on the treatment of the disease. Or at least the narrator does not tell us so. Isaiah proposes an empirical remedy from the healing lore of the time:

Isaiah told them to prepare a fig plaster; when it was made and applied to the inflammation, Hezekiah recovered (v. 21).

The narrator makes it obvious that he recovered. Did the plaster contain penicillin? Do figs have some natural power that we do not yet know about? Isaiah proceeds swiftly and naturally. He does not do anything spectacular or celebrate a recovery service. Although the narrator stresses the religious context, he does not speak of miracles. This is what interests us today.

Let us compare this scene with that of another king, who was also gravely ill:

Ahaziah fell through a latticed window in his roof-chamber in Samaria and injured himself (2 Kings 11:2). We may imagine him lying in bed suffering pain from fractures and haematomas perhaps, worried about the future of his kingdom. The king wants to know the outcome of the situation by a supernatural means. But instead of turning to the Lord God of Israel he resorts to the soothsayers of a foreign god:

He sent messengers to enquire of Baal-zebub the god of Ekron whether he would recover from this injury (v. 2).

Note. Baal-zebub is a malicious Hebrew deformation of a title of the Canaanite divinity. The original honorific title is Baal Zebul = Lord Prince. The Hebrew deformation is Baal Zebub = Lord of the flies. He is one of the many presences or local venerations of a Canaanite god, controller of meteors, fertility and thereby of life and death. The consultation is explicitly about the outcome of the disease. Perhaps it is also hoping for a possible cure. So the king is recognising the powers and competence of a foreign god, against the first commandment of the decalogue. He submits to the authority of an oracle, which Habakkuk mocks: 'It is only an image, a source of lies' (2:18).

Is there no God in Israel, that you send to enquire of Baal-zebub the god of Ekron? In consequence, you will not rise from the bed where you are lying; you will die (2 Kings 1:6).

Let us compare the two accounts. In our century medicine has made notable progress: in hygiene, diet, methods of diagnosis, pharmacopoeia and surgery. The average life span has increased by more than ten years. (Hezekiah is given fifteen extra years.) Infant mortality has decreased enormously. Diseases which used to be fatal have almost conventional remedies today . Many people of seventy today would not have reached this age in the last century. Many can look back on a shrewd diagnosis, efficacious treatment or successful operation. All this makes us accustomed to seeing these processes as natural, rather than religious. God's action is confined to miracles.

This is not the right way to look at things. God is no less active in the science of professors, the painstaking work in laboratories, the surgeons' skill, than when he works a miracle. The difference is that in the latter case he shows his hand. What we call natural is much more common than a miracle. If we look at it properly, it is no less admirable. Instead of doing miracles God gives powers to plants and intelligence and curiosity to human beings. Our self-preservation instinct, which sometimes leads us astray, is usually a dynamism set in us by God. The biblical text teaches us to look upwards, to put health and sickness back in their religious context. Ecclesiasticus (about a hundred and eighty years before Christ) with his good sense recommends us to do so in these words. Chapter 38:

[1]Value the services of a doctor
for he has his place assigned him by the Lord.
[2]His skill comes from the Most High,
and he is rewarded by kings.
[3]The doctor's knowledge gives him high standing
and wins him the admiration of the great.
[4]The Lord has created remedies from the earth,
and a sensible man will not disparage them.
[5]Was not water sweetened by a log,

and so the power of the Lord was revealed?
⁶The Lord has imparted knowledge to mortals,
that by their use of his marvels he may win praise;
⁷by means of them the doctor relieves pain
and from them the pharmacist compounds his
    mixture.
⁸There is no limit to the works of the Lord,
who spreads health over the whole world.
⁹My son, in time of illness do not be remiss,
but pray to the Lord and he will heal you.
¹⁰Keep clear of wrongdoing, amend your ways,
and cleanse your heart from all sin.
¹¹Bring a fragrant offering and a memorial sacrifice
    of flour;
pour oil on the sacrifice, be as lavish as you can.
¹²And the doctor should be called;
keep him by you for you need him also.
¹³A time may come when your recovery is in his
    hands;
¹⁴then he too will pray to the Lord
to grant success in relieving pain
and finding a cure to save the patient's life.
¹⁵He who sins before his Maker
shows himself arrogant before the doctor.

In the Old Testament God may have the title of doctor or healer as in 'I the LORD am your healer' (Ex 15:26) and 'healer of the broken-hearted' (Ps 147:3). Cardiologist would sound too clinical. But perhaps a member of this profession may like to give God this title. Psalm 103:3: 'He heals all my ills.' Nearly all the Old Testament texts that use the verb *rp'* (= heal, treat) have God as their subject. When they do not, they are in the negative. In a late and polemical text it is said of the king Asa:

Asa became gravely affected with disease in his feet; he did not seek guidance of the Lord but resorted to physicians (2 Chron 16:12).

Note. Perhaps the verb used, *drs,* has a religious meaning here. Or perhaps it does not refer to doctors but to healers using forbidden arts. The text does not make this clear. We are frequently told that God controls the process of health and sickness both ways:

Deut 32:39 I put to death and I keep alive,
            I inflict wounds and I heal.
Is 19:22   The LORD will strike down and then
            bring healing.
Is 30:26   The LORD binds up the broken limbs
            of his people and heals the wounds
            inflicted on them.
Hos 6:1   He has torn us, but he will heal us;
            he has wounded us, but he will bind up
            our wounds.

In the New Testament one of Jesus' activities is curing the sick, either provoking natural processes through faith or by working miracles. These cures can serve as a proof of his mission, as Luke relates:

When John was informed of all this by his disciples, he summoned two of them and sent them to the Lord with this question: 'Are you the one who is to come, or are we to expect someone else?' The men made their way to Jesus and said, 'John the Baptist has sent us to ask you, 'Are you the one who is to come, or are we to expect someone else?' There and then he healed many sufferers from diseases, plagues and evil spirits; and on many blind people he bestowed sight. Then he gave them this answer: 'Go an tell John what you have seen and heard: the blind regain their sight, the lame walk, lepers are made clean, the deaf hear, the dead are raised to life, the poor are brought good news' (Lk. 7:18-22)

Jesus passes his healing power on to his disciples. We read about some of their cures in the Acts of the Apostles. Later, miraculous cures become rare and the action of the glorified Christ can run through normal channels. Nevertheless Christ's power to heal diseases in an extraordinary way always remains present, both physical diseases and more frequently psychological and spiritual ones.

Paul says simply:

If we live, we live for the LORD,
If we die, we die for the LORD;
in life and in death we belong to the LORD.

Let us adapt this. If we are healthy, our health is for the Lord; if we are sick, our sickness is for the Lord. In health and in sickness we belong to the Lord. Jesus died in pain. The resurrection cures all his wounds, leaving marks as a memorial. Rising from the dead is the final cure.

Groups of leaders
Praising God

Before he dies Joshua gathers the people to give them his spiritual testament: Let them remember the past, or rather, the things God has done for them. Let them remain faithful to the Lord and the covenant, not contaminate themselves with idolatry and other nations' perversions. Obviously the author (the Deuteronomist) puts one of his sermons into the mouth of the dying Joshua. The fact that the speech is conventional and familiar does not mean it is not also true and valid. Then we pass on to a brief note at the end of the book of Joshua:

> Israel served the LORD throughout the lifetime of Joshua and of the elders who outlived him and who knew all that the LORD had done for Israel (24:21).

The same sentence is repeated in Judges 2:7. It stresses the importance of memory and Joshua's witness. The elders together form a college which is like an official body of witnesses. They bear witness to what they have *seen and heard*. What God has done for his people becomes a present force through conviction and public witness. In the body of elders the past goes on living. It has nothing to do with senile ramblings about their own past exploits: 'When I was young, in my day...' The biblical elders are not witnesses to their own former greatness, to better times, but to God's own deeds. Having seen and been present at God's great interventions in history is not just a privilege. There is a responsibility to bear witness. If a Christian has lived his life with full awareness, sharing in the Church's life, he will have something to tell, quite a lot. He cannot keep it to himself. I have the feeling that we often live a sort of everyday Christianity lacking in fervour or clarity. Even though we may meet God in our daily lives, we lack a wide historical horizon. Bearing witness in this sense is not retreating into the past but powerfully bringing the past into the present. For this, old people are called upon not to keep silent.

Let us look at another case, centuries later, in which the elders as a group are invited to give their opinion and advice. We read about it in the First Book of Kings, in the dramatic episode of the schism. According to the biblical account Solomon had promoted the economic and cultural development of his nation. In three stages Saul-David-Solomon-Israel had gone from being a besieged and powerless people to becoming a prosperous kingdom highly respected at home and abroad. Many were proud of their country and their king, and the biblical text witnesses to their uncritical enthusiasm. Because obviously Solomon had fostered the development by means of heavy taxes, forced loans and splendid luxury at court. The enthusiasm of some was countered by the discontent of many others. This is the situation facing Solomon's successor. The heir is Rehoboam. A first significant fact is that in order to be proclaimed king Rehoboam has to go to Shechem, the ancient tribal capital in the centre or north of the country. Not David's still recent capital Jerusalem. Rehoboam is proclaimed king in Shechem (1 Kings 12). Immediately the people's representatives come to the young king with an urgent petition:

Your father laid a harsh yoke upon us; but if you will now lighten the harsh labour he imposed and the heavy yoke he laid on us, we shall serve you (1 Kings 12:4).

Before replying Rehoboam asks for time to consult and he engages in two rounds of consultation. First he consults the elders, then the young. Note it is not a question of simply opposing young and old, as if the old were the good and the young the bad ones. The elders provide historical experience placed at the service of politics. Indeed the elders, or at least some of them, can remember the simple and relatively austere life under David and the beginning of Solomon's reign. They can compare that simple state of well-being with the oppressive opulence of the present. The young men Rehoboam consults are a particular group: the young men who *had grown up with him*. That is, those who had grown up enjoying the privileged court life-style based on exploitation of the people. It is significant that the leader of the rebellion should have been a leader of the gangs of workers, obliged to render a service which today we would call forced labour. The elders know different epochs and they appreciate the opposing factors in the present situation. The young men who are consulted know neither what things were like before nor the real situation of the proletariat. The elders advise the king to give in:

If today you are willing to serve this people, show yourself their servant now and speak kindly to them, and they will be your servants ever after (v. 7).

The young men advise another turn of the screw: repression as a counter-measure to the people's petitions. The text of their reply gives in imaginative language a programme for despotic rule:

> My little finger is thicker than my father's loins. My father laid a heavy yoke on you, but I shall make it heavier. My father whipped you, but I shall flay you (v. 10).

We cannot quote this text as an example of a generation battle, because the two groups are precisely qualified and do not represent the general rule. The elders want to put a stop to a dangerous and unjust process. They listen to the people's voice and channel it to the king. Taking the side of the poor, they are more progressive than a group of spoilt young men, who are anxious to preserve their own privileges. Old age of course does not automatically bring discernment. Rehoboam gives the elders a consultative vote and then ignores it. They have fulfilled their responsibility. They are judged by history and God's word through the prophet: 'This is my doing' (12:24).

The relationship between old and young can become generational with reference to the future. Then tension may arise between particular age groups because of a radically new historical situation. Malachi, or the protagonist of his book, is considered to be the last of the prophets. Following an ancient tradition, many Bibles place the short book of Malachi — four chapters — in the block of Minor Prophets, after Daniel. In the history of Hebrew thought Malachi is the last prophet, and Daniel represents something new, the apocalypse.

Malachi, the last prophet, looks back to the first, Elijah, who was snatched up into heaven and kept there waiting for a new mission that will be more important than the first. The last words in the book of Malachi are these:

Look, I shall send you the prophet Elijah before the great and terrible day of the LORD comes. He will reconcile parents to their children and children to their parents, lest I come and put the land under a ban to destroy it (Mal 4:5).

Confronted with the decisive event, it is taken for granted that the generations divide and oppose one another, seeming to break down national unity. The parents belong to the old regime; they are the bearers and guardians of sacred traditions. The children are ready to jump forward, cross the river to enter on a new stage of history. They fight against their parents' stubbornness with youthful impatience, the solidity of the past clashes with the fluidity of the present. The tension must be resolved not by a break but by reconciliation. Elijah, the old and the new, will be the minister of this reconciliation. In his time Elijah was both old and new, a Moses come back to life who met God on Mount Horeb. With centuries of inactive waiting one would surmise he has accumulated experience. Now they are sending him for a new mission: to save the past without closing off access to the imminent future; to open the doors to the future without closing those to the past; reconcile parents with children, children with parents. There is a need to embrace both horizons, this is his special mission: I will send *you*.

Perhaps two centuries pass until in about 180 BC a teacher called Jesus Ben Sirach takes up the theme in the following words:

Scripture records that you are to come at the appointed time to allay the divine wrath before it erupts in fury, to reconcile father and son, and to restore the tribes of Jacob (Eccles 48:10).

In the text we possess Ben Sirach has left out one phrase and only mentions the reconciliation between

174

parents and children. As if it were the parents who unjustly and dangerously resist novelty, as if they were trying to hold back the glorious future. Perhaps the parents have failed and it is the children who are called to *restore the tribes of Jacob*.

When at last the moment foretold and long awaited comes, and John the son of Zechariah becomes the new Elijah, his old father receives a message from an angel:

He will go before him as forerunner, possessed by the spirit and power of Elijah, to reconcile father and child, to convert the rebellious to the ways of the righteous, to prepare a people that shall be fit for the Lord (Lk 1:17).

Luke quotes the limited version from Ecclesiasticus.

Zechariah bending over his son John, who will become the Baptist, is another in our series of old people. But at the moment I am concerned with groups of elders, as a class or generation. For many old people resist the youthful novelty of Jesus of Nazareth.

Jesus is young, his friends and intimate companions are young, the Baptist was young. Standing opposite and against Jesus we frequently find a group called 'the elders.' True, in the Bible this is more the name of an office than an age description. But often the two are combined. Moreover it is interesting that the name of the office is connected with age. Jesus' contact with the 'elders' is often polemical. Among countless examples I shall pick out a number of texts in which these elders (*presbyteroi*) act:

They asked him: 'Why do your disciples break the ancient traditions? They do not wash their hands before eating?' He answered them: 'And what about you? Why do you break God's commandment in the interest of your tradition?' (Mt 15:2).

From that time Jesus began to make it clear to his disciples that he had to go to Jerusalem, and endure great suffering at the hands of the elders, chief priests and scribes (Mt 16:21).

He entered the temple, and as he was teaching, the chief priests and elders of the nation came up to him and asked: 'By what authority are you acting like this? Who gave you this authority?' (Mt 21:23).

The elders play a prominent part in the accounts of the passion. When it is not a question of persons but of things, values, institutions, the adjectives used are: 'old and new.' Let us read the classic text in Luke's version:

No one tears a piece from a new garment to patch an old one; if he does, he will have made a hole in the new garment, and the patch taken from the new will not match the old. No one puts new wine into old wineskins; if he does, the new wine will burst the skins and the wine will spill out, and the skins be ruined. New wine goes into fresh skins! And no one after drinking old wine wants new; for he says, 'The old wine is good' (Lk. 5:36-39).

In the face of Christ's newness and youth, conversion and reconciliation have a single direction: parents with children, old with young, old with new. But now Jesus Christ has come and we want to be faithful to his past. Jesus Christ died young and rose from the dead young to remain young for centuries and centuries. Old people always have to reconcile themselves with his inexhaustible youth and newness. The Church is Christ's body, which goes on growing throughout history. There are old people who want to restrict Christ's growth to a preceding stage of Church history, in the name of their routines. They shut the door against anything new. They are like the 'elders' in the gospels.

176

Another correlative use of the adjective 'old' is to be found in two letters of St Paul, to the Ephesians and Colossians:

> Renouncing your former way of life, you must lay aside the old human nature which, deluded by its desires, is in process of decay; you must be renewed in mind and spirit and put on the new nature created in God's likeness, which shows itself in the upright and devout life called for by the truth (Eph 4:22).

> Do not lie to one another, now that you have discarded the old human nature and the conduct that goes with it, and have put on the new nature which is constantly being renewed in the image of its Creator (Col 3:9).

Both texts refer to human nature created in God's image. Imagine Adam newly created, young, glowing, perfect — like the beloved in the Song of Songs. Like a new minted coin or medal he bears the imprint of God's image. With the passage of time and sin the image grows fainter, begins to be obliterated. It is to be melted down and re-struck using a perfect exemplar as its model. It is melted down in the crucible of repentance. The perfect exemplar is Jesus Christ and it is new, minted by the Holy Spirit. We too will one day be born anew and we are developing towards radiant youth.

Let us look at the spiritual order: baptism; childhood innocence, lost and regained; a modelling process that goes on for years because God's image is not complete in us. When at the end of the road we meet Jesus our brother, the perfect exemplar, shall we be like him? If he takes us by the hand and asks us: 'Who is this *the image of?*', what shall we reply? Let us hope that one day our old age will be transformed into newness, a renewed and perfected image of an original creation.

Is God old or new? Daniel the seer imagines him thus:

> As I was looking, thrones were set in place and the Ancient in Years took his seat; his robe was white as snow, his hair like lamb's wool (Dan 7:9).

On another occasion he is called the 'Ancient of Days.' Because he is before all ages we imagine him as old. But if the years do not pass for him we may also imagine him as young. Really, neither one nor the other, as he is above such distinctions. However if we are to imagine him I think we should imagine him as ever new, because his fullness is inexhaustible. Let us try and meditate on God's perpetual newness, to see if we can be infected by it in spite of our age.

You see, God is new and in order to reveal this aspect of himself to us he presents himself as what is newest in humanity: a baby. Even though there may be several children in a family, every child that is born is new. There is nothing newer than a baby: he inaugurates his own new era, he is a bundle of possibilities. If anything is repeated it is in a new way. So in the baby's prodigious newness God enables us to glimpse his own perpetual newness.

We too have to become like children again in order to enter the kingdom of heaven. We should not become infantile – old age as second childhood – but recover or cultivate our capacity for discovery and surprise. It is not true that we have already seen everything. There are still so many things to be discovered. If we do not think of ourselves as protagonists, let us at least be spectators and participants.

Curiosity is a sign of spiritual youth. Senility loses interest in everything. Curiosity is the desire to know what we do not know. As the world of our ignorance is so immense we have to restrict our curiosity to certain fields. Defining these fields is important because not all equally demand our attention, or because some are better suited than others to our temperament and education. But even when we have defined a reasonable sphere for our curiosity let us leave doors open for festive escapes. Curiosity sharpens the attention. Modern science keeps on extending our knowledge more and more, so that there is always more for us to learn. Old people are happy if they keep an active curiosity in science, the arts, history or other people. Or in the wonderful works of God. One day, which is coming nearer and nearer, we will be filled with his presence.

There is one more group of elders in the last book of the Bible, Revelation. In spite of the difficulties about the form and style of this book, we can get certain things from it. Above all, the elders are present and active in the Bible, from Genesis to Revelation. There is no discrimination or confinement.

The seer of Revelation describes a heavenly court and in it there is a sort of senate. We know that the word 'senate' (*senatus*) comes from the Latin for old person = *senex*. That is, originally the word referred to old age and later came to signify an important office. The heavenly senate consists of twenty-four elders, the combined number of the twelve tribes of Israel and the twelve apostles, as representing the Old and the New Testament. But as senators they represent everyone. If there is any preference in heaven, the author gives it to these elders (in accordance with his culture). A senate on earth normally has a governing function: it deliberates and decides. Let us look at the activity of this heavenly senate, especially in chapters 4 and 5. In the vision God appears as a majestic king sitting on his shining throne:

In the circle about this throne were twenty-four other thrones, and on them were seated twenty-four elders, robed in white and wearing gold crowns... (4:4).

The twenty-four elders prostrate themselves before the One who sits on the throne and they worship him who lives for ever and ever. As they lay their crowns before the throne they cry: 'You are worthy, O Lord our God, to receive glory and honour and power, because you created all things; by your will they were created and have their being!' (4:10).

These heavenly senators' function is not to deliberate or advise, but to 'praise and worship.' Casting down their crowns expresses the creature's profound respect for the Creator and their words utter his praise. They praise him for the creation, of which the elders are part and become representatives, and 'through their voice the other creatures.' Creation is so abundant that they can praise for centuries without repeating themselves, always singing a new song. Creation is so admirable that only in heaven can it worthily be praised. Praise begun on earth is taken up into the heavenly liturgy.

In Revelation chapter 5 another person appears: the Lamb. An emblematic name meaning he was gentle and sacrificed. The elders are to praise him and offer the prayers of the elect in golden bowls:

The four living creatures and the twenty-four elders prostrated themselves before the Lamb. Each of the elders had a harp; they held golden bowls full of incense, the prayers of God's people, and they were singing a new song: You are worthy to receive the scroll and break its seals, for you were slain and by your blood you bought for God people of every tribe and language, nation and race. You have made them a royal house of priests for our God, and they shall reign on earth (Rev 5:8-9).

Petition goes with praise, petition for protection and favours. The heavenly worshippers do not need to ask for anything, praising is enough. But through their earlier experience and the position they occupy the senators transmit to the Lamb the prayers of the companions. And they sing a new song, for the redemption. By his sacrifice the Lamb has gathered a new universal people of God. Only in heaven can the full richness of the redemption be comprehended and it will be fullness of joy to understand it and praise it.

The heavenly liturgy is answered by the cosmic liturgy. By which the elders fulfil another function, which is to initiate and preside over the universal song of praise to God: 'Human beings are created to praise God':

> Then I heard all created things, in heaven, on earth, under the earth, and in the sea, crying: 'Praise and honour, glory and might, to him who sits on the throne and to the Lamb for ever' (Rev 5:13).

Praising God, presenting prayers, directing the cosmic praise: the elders in heaven perform no small function.

Paul
Be acceptable to God
at all times

When Paul wrote his second letter to the community at Corinth (we leave aside the problem of the two letters), he was probably sixty years old. Such an age in ancient times would have placed him in the category of *presbyteroi* (which is coming close to our retirement age). Paul does not retire voluntarily. He will be partly retired by prison and finally by death. At his age Paul was still in full spate of apostolic activity, but his mind could wander off onto his personal future. He does not mind tribulations and sufferings because they are part of an apostle's life; they can help him raise his hope. Paul begins his exposition with a series of opposites:

No wonder we do not lose heart! Though our outward humanity is in decay, yet day by day we are inwardly renewed. Our troubles are slight and short-lived, and their outcome is an eternal glory which far outweighs them, provided our eyes are fixed, not on the things that are seen, but on the things that are unseen; for what is seen is transient, what is unseen is eternal (2 Cor 4:16).

The series of contrasts goes: outward/inward; decay/renewal; short-lived/eternal; slight/overwhelming; transient/eternal; seen/unseen. What is seen is here and now, a human being subject to decay, principally evident in the body, but also in functions and activities we call spiritual, like the power of concentration, mental agility, remembering recent dates, resistance, creativity... Decay comes from our natural human condition. In Paul's case there is also the struggle and pains of being an apostle. Inwardly there is the Christian dedicated to God, aware and responsible. Physical and mental decay is evident at his age and is increased by his continual struggles. Paul is immersed in this visible world around him in which he works. He sees it and touches it and communicates with it. But his mind focuses and concentrates on the transcendent world which is revealed to the inward gaze of faith and hope. So two opposite movements are operating at once: one descending, irreparably, and the other ascending day by day. The upward movement will win. The troubles do not matter if their outcome is an eternal glory which far outweighs them. If what is seen is glorious, what is unseen is even more so. The transient will be succeeded by the lasting. It is not difficult to apply Paul's teaching to ourselves.

In the following paragraphs of the letter Paul intertwines another series of contrasts using three metaphors. Clothes: naked/clothed/reclothed; housing: tent/building/dwelling; place of residence: home/exile. The first two metaphors are mixed and may confuse us in the next paragraph. The substance is: Let us yearn for the happy lasting life, but without losing the one we have now. We should like the one to come to be a gentle continuation, something that is added and placed on top without destroying the previous life.

We know that if the earthly frame that houses us today is demolished, we possess a building which God has provided — a house not made by human hands, eternal and in heaven. In this present body we groan, yearning to be covered by our heavenly habitation put on over this one, in the hope that, being thus clothed we shall not find ourselves naked. We groan indeed, we who are enclosed within this earthly frame; we are oppressed because we do not want to have the old body stripped off. What we want is to be covered by the new body put on over it, so that our mortality may be absorbed into life immortal. It is for this destiny that God himself has been shaping us; and as a pledge of it he has given us the Spirit (2 Cor 5: 1-5).

It is as if the body were a provisional tent, where we camp until the time comes to move to a permanent building or habitation. Like people living in huts or cabins after a disaster. Or like something we wear. In order to move to the permanent dwelling we have to abandon the tent. In order to put on the glory dress, we have to take off the dress that is falling to pieces. If we yearn for it, it is because we think of it as real because someone has awakened our awareness of it. It is not a house built by human hands or a dress of human weaving. We are destined to receive immortality as a gift of God through the action of the Spirit. Let us allow the Spirit to breathe into our mind, awaken our longing. Let the Spirit begin stripping us and making us ready.

The third paragraph is easier. The human being living in the body lives in exile from his country. He has to strip off the body in order to be with the Lord. Body means everything bodily, including the mind conditioned by being in the body. Our imagination is fed by our bodily senses, our ideas depend on sensations to make the leap, and we often think about bodily realities. Our desires are directed towards things of the body or go through them and beyond. When we strip off all this will we be naked, pure spirit? No, it will be like putting on another body and we shall live in the Lord's country.

Therefore we never cease to be confident. We know that so long as we are at home in the body we are exiles from the Lord; faith is our guide, not sight. We are confident, I say, and would rather be exiled from the body and make our home with the Lord. That is why it is our ambition, wherever we are, at home or in exile, to be acceptable to him. For we must all have our lives laid open before the tribunal of Christ, where each must receive what is due to him for his conduct in the body, good or bad (2 Cor 5: 6-10).

One phrase in this third paragraph guides us towards another famous passage of Paul's which we meditated on in Part 1 and is to be found in the Letter to the Philippians. In the middle of his work Paul feels pulled two ways by opposite forces: upwards towards the Lord, like a force of gravity lodged in his will. And pulled back by his apostolic work and the good of his people. Who can do more? (Phil 1:21). Paul's exact age does not matter much. His teaching and example both apply to the old.

Nicodemus
A new and everlasting life

No one says that Nicodemus was old. But as he himself refers to old age, we are going to give him a place in our meditation. He is a Pharisee, who knows the Law, *a master in Israel*. He had a certain position, and was honest and open. He recognises the value of this new itinerant teacher called Jesus of Nazareth. He asks for an appointment with him by night. Why by night? John leaves it up to us to think of plausible motives. For example, Jesus is very busy during the day and has to use the night for prayer and personal interviews. Or perhaps it is some Old Testament reminiscence of nocturnal teaching:

> In the night he imparts wisdom to my inmost being (Ps 16:7).

There is Jacob's vision or dream at night in Genesis 28 and 31:24. Solomon's in 1 Kings 3:5; Job's in 4:13.

Or perhaps it is for the immediate context, because the passage ends with the theme of light: *light has come into the world, but people preferred darkness to light*.

Jesus immediately states his radical requirement. You have to be born again to enter the kingdom of God. Being born does not mean improving yourself but beginning a new existence. We know what the phrase 'from my mother's womb' meant for the Hebrews: birth defines nature and destiny. In order to be citizens of the new kingdom you have to be born into it, because only birth gives the right of citizenship. Here the narrator makes Nicodemus not understand, so that we may understand better:

> 'But how can someone be born when he is old?' asked Nicodemus. 'Can he enter his mother's womb a second time and be born?' (Jn 3:4).

Even an adolescent or a child could not go back into the mother's womb. Nicodemus' question puts the extreme case: an old person has already lived his life, defined his destiny. It remains for him to be 'gathered to his own' (according to the Hebrew euphemism). Perhaps Nicodemus makes another mistake: 'enter *his* mother's womb again.' If it is *his* mother, the new birth will repeat and not change anything. In the Old Testament we do not find even a remote antecedent for such a miracle: being born again. Some children are restored to life (legends of Elijah and Elisha). An epic song declares in a moment of exaltation that Joshua ordered the sun to stand still (Josh 10), stopping time, but not making it go backwards. The shadow goes backwards on Hezekiah's steps that told the time (Is 38).

Jesus corrects Nicodemus and continues. I am speaking of a real birth and natural birth is an appropriate image for it. Not from your mother's womb, but from another mother, which is water made fertile by the Spirit. The baptismal font is the Church's maternal womb, made fertile by the Spirit of Christ. Whoever is born from it receives this new nature: *Flesh can give birth only to flesh; it is Spirit that gives birth to spirit*. And isn't this birth more miraculous than the one Nicodemus objects to? Yes, because God's creative power is at work in it. The Spirit hovers over the waters, transforming chaos into cosmos. The Spirit penetrates the water, making it fertile and bringing a new birth, a new creature.

In applying this teaching to themselves old people

might have this objection. We have already been born again in baptism. Can we be reborn? We are not anabaptists. What can an old person do? Let us look at two ways out: renewal and resurrection. Both use the morpheme re-.

Firstly, let us return spiritually to the waters of baptism as a spring of life, to recover strength and vitality: *he leads me to water where I may rest; he revives my spirit* (Ps 23:3). Let us go to Christ's side from which living water flows. Being born means opening up to innumerable possibilities: a child can learn any language spoken where it grows up. That is, it is possible for any language to become the child's own but not all. The child will fulfil some of these possibilities and not others. Language is just one example. He can learn a second, third, etcetera, throughout life. Every stage of life presents an array of possibilities. Old age too. At age seventy or more there are still many things to do: new knowledge to gain, actions, experiences. If being born means beginning, every new beginning is a bit like birth.

In his *Life of Moses* Gregory of Nyssa says that anything that is subject to change is in a certain sense continually being born. And he adds that in a way we are our own parents, we give birth to ourselves by free choice. This is more certain in the kingdom of the Spirit: although an old person cannot go back into his or her mother's womb, the Spirit can still renew.

Secondly, it is legitimate and biblical to think of the resurrection as a symbol of birth. The Greek word *prototokos* means first-born (*tiktein* = to give birth). So, Jesus is the first-born of creation, the first-born of humanity. He is also the first-born from the dead through his resurrection. Look at the following texts:

He is the image of the invisible God, the first-born of all creation (Col 1:15).

For those whom God knew before ever they were, he also ordained to share the likeness of his Son, so that he might be the first-born among a large family of brothers (Rom 8:29).

He is the beginning, the first-born from the dead (the first to be born from death) (Col 1:18).

Jesus Christ, the faithful witness, the first-born from the dead (Rev 1:5).

In the last two of the above quotations the Greek uses the preposition *ek*, which means 'from where', suggesting that the risen Christ is born as the first from the place of death. We find the term *prototokos* in Luke 2:7: *Mary gave birth to a son, her first-born*. And hence we have the symbolism used by the Fathers of the Church: as Jesus was the first to be born of Mary, he is also the first to be born from the womb of death. He comes from Mary's intact womb and he comes out of the sepulchre newly-excavated in the rock. The sepulchre is like the womb of mother earth. He is born to live and die, he rises again and is reborn to live for ever.

So, Jesus Christ is the first-born among many because he communicates the *power of his resurrection* (Phil 3:10) to those who believe in him, his brothers and sisters. By the power of the Spirit he makes them be born again for everlasting life. Thus we read in the great eschatology in the book of Isaiah. First he announces that *the LORD will destroy death for ever* (25:8). Further on he explains this using and transforming a tradition symbol in several cultures:

^{26:19}But your dead will live, their bodies will rise
again.
Those who sleep in the earth will awake and shout
for joy;
for your dew is a dew of sparkling light,
and the earth will bring those long dead to birth
again.

Mother earth, which jealously holds the bodies of the dead, is made pregnant by the shining dew from heaven. She enters into a trance and gives birth to the dead, alive again. Resurrection means being born again for a new and lasting life.

So now shall we repeat Nicodemus' objection? An old person cannot be born again, cannot enter his mother's womb again to be reborn. No, an old person will enter the womb of our common mother the earth by death, and be reborn by the power of the Spirit.

If the Spirit of him who raised Jesus from the dead dwells in you, then the God who raised Christ from the dead will also give new life to your mortal bodies through his indwelling Spirit (Rom 8:11).

An old person can and will be born again. It is the mystery of hope, which many do not understand because they do not have faith. It is because:

The wind blows where it wills; you hear the sound of it, but you do not know where it comes from or where it is going. So it is with everyone who is born from the Spirit (Jn 3:8).

But anyone who believes and hopes does know where he comes from and where he is going.
On the other hand:

In the eyes of the foolish they seemed to be dead; their departure was reckoned as defeat, and their going from us as a disaster. But they are in peace (Wis 3:2).

Nicodemus came to talk to Jesus by night. Night is falling in our lives and we go to talk with Jesus, because he came down from heaven to teach us the doctrine of rebirth, which is a heavenly doctrine:

'You a teacher of Israel and ignorant of such things!' said Jesus. 'In very truth I tell you, we speak of what we know, and testify to what we have seen...' (Jn 3:10).

'No one has gone up into heaven except the one who came down from heaven' (v. 13).

'God so loved the world that he gave his only Son, that everyone who has faith in him may not perish but have everlasting life' (v. 16).